For Exams Scheduled After June 30, 2018

FINAL REVIEW
BUSINESS

UPDATES AND ACADEMIC HELP
Click on Customer and Academic Support under CPA Resources at
http://www.becker.com/cpa-review.html

CUSTOMER SERVICE AND TECHNICAL SUPPORT
Call 1-877-CPA-EXAM (outside the U.S. +1-630-472-2213)
or click Customer and Academic Support under CPA Resources at
http://www.becker.com/cpa-review.html

This textbook contains information that was current at the time of printing.
Your course software will be updated on a regular basis as the content
that is tested on the CPA Exam evolves and as we improve our materials.
Note the version reference below and click on Customer and Academic
Support under CPA Resources at http://www.becker.com/cpa-review.html
for a list of available updates or to learn if a newer version of this book is
available to be ordered.

V 3.1

BECKER
PROFESSIONAL EDUCATION®

COURSE DEVELOPMENT TEAM

Timothy F. Gearty, CPA, MBA, JD . . . . Editor in Chief, Financial/Regulation (Tax) National Editor
Angeline S. Brown, CPA, MAC . . . . Sr. Director, Product Management
Valerie Funk Anderson, CPA . . . . Sr. Manager, Accounting Curriculum
Stephen Bergens, CPA . . . . Manager, Accounting Curriculum
Patrice W. Johnson, CPA . . . . Sr. Manager, Accounting Curriculum
Tom Cox, CPA, CMA . . . . Financial (GASB & NFP) National Editor
Steven J. Levin, JD . . . . Regulation (Law) National Editor
Pete Console . . . . Sr. Director, Educational Technologies
Brian Cave . . . . Sr. Manager, Software Development
Dan Corrales . . . . Sr. Manager, Curriculum Quality Assurance
Danita De Jane . . . . Director, Course Development
Anson Miyashiro . . . . Manager, Product Development
John Ott . . . . Manager, Visual Design
Tim Munson . . . . Team Lead, Product Development
Linda Finestone . . . . Sr. Course Editor
Naomi Oseida . . . . Product Development
Eric Vasquez . . . . Product Development

CONTRIBUTING EDITORS

Teresa C. Anderson, CPA, CMA, MPA

Katie Barnette, CPA

Jim DeSimpelare, CPA, MBA

Melisa F. Galasso, CPA

Holly Hawk, CPA, CGMA

Julie D. McGinty, CPA

Sandra McGuire, CPA, MBA

Stephanie Morris, CPA, MAcc

Michelle Moshe, CPA, DipIFR

Peter Olinto, JD, CPA

Sandra Owen, CPA, MBA, JD

Michelle M. Pace, CPA

Jennifer J. Rivers, CPA

Josh Rosenberg, MBA, CPA, CFA, CFP

Jonathan R. Rubin, CPA, MBA

Michael Rybak, CPA, CFA

Denise M. Stefano, CPA, CGMA, MBA

Elizabeth Lester Walsh, CPA, CITP

Permissions

Material from *Uniform CPA Examination Selected Questions and Unofficial Answers*, 1989–2018, copyright © by American Institute of Certified Public Accountants, Inc., is reprinted and/or adapted with permission.

Any knowing solicitation or disclosure of any questions or answers included on any CPA Examination is prohibited.

LICENSE AGREEMENT—TERMS & CONDITIONS

DO NOT DOWNLOAD, ACCESS, AND/OR USE ANY OF THESE MATERIALS (AS THAT TERM IS DEFINED BELOW) UNTIL YOU HAVE READ THIS LICENSE AGREEMENT CAREFULLY. IF YOU DOWNLOAD, ACCESS, AND/OR USE ANY OF THESE MATERIALS, YOU ARE AGREEING AND CONSENTING TO BE BOUND BY AND ARE BECOMING A PARTY TO THIS LICENSE AGREEMENT ("AGREEMENT").

The printed Materials provided to you and/or the Materials provided for download to your computer and/or provided via a web application to which you are granted access are NOT for sale and are not being sold to you. You may NOT transfer these Materials to any other person or permit any other person to use these Materials. You may <u>only</u> acquire a license to use these Materials and <u>only</u> upon the terms and conditions set forth in this Agreement. Read this Agreement carefully <u>before</u> downloading, and/or accessing, and/or using these Materials. <u>Do not</u> download and/or access, and/or use these Materials <u>unless</u> you agree with all terms of this Agreement.

NOTE: You may already be a party to this Agreement if you registered for a Becker Professional Education CPA Final Review program (the "Program") or placed an order for these Materials online or using a printed form that included this License Agreement. Please review the termination section regarding your rights to terminate this License Agreement and receive a refund of your payment.

Grant: Upon your acceptance of the terms of this Agreement, in a manner set forth above, Becker Professional Development Corporation ("Becker") hereby grants to you a non-exclusive, revocable, non-transferable, non-sublicensable, limited license to use (as defined below) the Materials by downloading them onto a computer and/or by accessing them via a web application using a user ID and password (as defined below), and any Materials to which you are granted access as a result of your license to use these Materials and/or in connection with the Program on the following terms:

During the Term (as defined below) of this Agreement, you may:

• use the Materials for preparation for one or more parts of the CPA exam (the "Exam"), and/or for your studies relating to the subject matter covered by the Program and/or the Exam), and/or for your studies relating to the subject matter covered by the Materials and/or the Exam, including taking electronic and/or handwritten notes during the Program, provided that all notes taken that relate to the subject matter of the Materials are and shall remain Materials subject to the terms of this Agreement;

• download the Materials onto any single device;

• download the Materials onto a second device so long as the first device and the second device are not used simultaneously;

• download the Materials onto a third device so long as the first, second, and third device are not used simultaneously; and

• download the Materials onto a fourth device so long as the first, second, third, and fourth device are not used simultaneously.

The number of installations may vary outside of the U.S. Please review your local office policies and procedures to confirm the number of installations granted—your local office's policies and procedures regarding the number of allowable activations of downloads supersedes the limitations contained herein and is controlling.

You may not:

• use the Materials for any purpose other than as expressly permitted above;

• use the downloaded Materials on more than one device, computer terminal, or workstation at the same time;

• make copies of the Materials;

• rent, lease, license, lend, or otherwise transfer or provide (by gift, sale, or otherwise) all or any part of the Materials to anyone;

• permit the use of all or any part of the Materials by anyone other than you; or

• reverse engineer, decompile, disassemble, or create derivate works of the Materials.

Materials: As used in this Agreement, the term "Materials" means and includes any printed materials provided to you by Becker, and/or to which you are granted access by Becker (directly or indirectly) in connection with your license of the Materials and/or the Program, and shall include notes you take (by hand, electronically, digitally, or otherwise) while using the Materials relating to the subject matter of the Materials; any and all electronically-stored/accessed/delivered, and/or digitally-stored/accessed/delivered materials included under this License via download to a computer or via access to a web application, and/or otherwise provided to you and/or to which you are otherwise granted access by Becker (directly or indirectly), including, but not limited to, applications downloadable from a third party, for example Google® or Amazon®, in connection with your license of the Materials.

Title: Becker is and will remain the owner of all title, ownership rights, intellectual property, and all other rights and interests in and to the Materials that are subject to the terms of this Agreement. The Materials are protected by the copyright laws of the United States and international copyright laws and treaties.

Use of Navigator 2.0: If your employer or college/university has instructed Becker to use its Navigator 2.0 to track your studies, the following will occur: a) once you have activated your software (course log-in), you will be asked to set up your study planner. In order to do this, you may be required to provide information about yourself as part of the Program registration process, or as part of your continued use of the Materials. You agree that any registration information you give to Becker will be shared by Becker with your employer or college/university ; and b) once that is done, Navigator 2.0 will automatically track if you are behind in your studies based on your study planner, your office location, your service line within the firm, your college/university course, which course parts were purchased (Audit and Attestation, Financial Accounting and Reporting, Business Environment and Concepts, and Regulation), what format are you using (online, live, self-study), your course progress, study time details (hours/min in course, # of log-ins, last log in), exam progress details including: whether you applied to take the exam, and if so, the state to which you applied; whether you received your NTS (notice to schedule), and if so, its expiration date; whether you scheduled your exam, and if so, the date; whether you received any scores and what they were; and the number of attempts to pass each of the four parts.

Navigator 2.0 Liability Provisions: You hereby waive any claims, causes of action, and damages, and agree to hold harmless and indemnify Becker and its affiliates, officers, agents, and employees from any claim, suit or action arising from or related to your use of the Materials, the sharing of any of your information by Becker with your employer or violation of these terms, including any liability or expense arising from claims, losses, damages, suits, judgments, litigation costs and attorneys' fees.

SUBJECT TO THE OVERALL PROVISION ABOVE, YOU EXPRESSLY UNDERSTAND AND AGREE THAT BECKER, ITS PARENT CORPORATION, SUBSIDIARIES AND AFFILIATES, AND THE OFFICERS, AGENTS AND EMPLOYEES OF THOSE ENTITIES, SHALL NOT BE LIABLE TO YOU FOR ANY LOSS OR DAMAGE THAT MAY BE INCURRED BY YOU, INCLUDING BUT NOT LIMITED TO LOSS OR DAMAGE AS A RESULT BECKER SHARING YOUR INFORMATION WITH YOUR EMPLOYER OR COLLEGE/UNIVERSITY.

THE LIMITATIONS ON BECKER'S LIABILITY TO YOU IN THE PARAGRAPHS ABOVE SHALL APPLY WHETHER OR NOT BECKER HAS BEEN ADVISED OF OR SHOULD HAVE BEEN AWARE OF THE POSSIBILITY OF ANY SUCH LOSSES ARISING.

Termination: The license granted under this Agreement commences upon your receipt of these Materials. This license shall terminate the earlier of: (i) ten (10) business days after notice to you of non-payment of or default on any payment due Becker which has not been cured within such 10-day period; or (ii) immediately if you fail to comply with any of the limitations described above; or (iii) upon expiration of the period ending eighteen (18) months after you log-in to access the Materials, that is, the first time you visit the Becker Program homepage and log-in using your user identification and password; or upon expiration of the twenty-four (24) month period beginning upon your purchase of the Material, whichever of these periods first transpires (the "Term"). In addition, upon termination of this license for any reason, you must delete or otherwise remove from your computer and other device any Materials you downloaded, including, but not limited to, any archival copies you may have made. The Title, Exclusion of Warranties, Exclusion of Damages, Indemnification and Remedies, Severability of Terms and Governing Law provisions, and any amounts due, shall survive termination of the license.

Your Limited Right to Terminate this License and Receive a Refund: You may terminate this license for the in-class, online, and self-study Programs in accordance with Becker's refund policy as provided below.

Cancellations and Refunds: To cancel your enrollment and receive a refund, contact Becker Professional Education at 800-868-3900.

Textbooks should be returned within 10 days of notification of withdrawal. Students should contact Becker for a "Return Materials Authorization" number prior to shipping returns. Students should ship materials by certified mail or an alternative traceable method. Flashcards and the material license fees for the Becker Promise are non-refundable. The cost to return materials is the responsibility of the student. Refunds will be made within 30 days from the date of cancellation. Non-receipt of shipment disputes must be made with 90 days of original purchase date.

All returns must be sent to: Becker Professional Education.
Attn: Becker Returns, 200 Finn Ct., Farmingdale NY, 11735

For **Online CPA Exam Review Course and CPA Final Review course students***, a full tuition refund (less any applicable savings and fees) will be issued within 10 days of initial purchase or first login, whichever comes first.

For **Live Format and Cohort Program CPA Review students***, a full tuition refund (minus all applicable savings) will be issued to students who withdraw on or before the 5th business day or if students do not attend any part of the course (no-shows) after the start date of the scheduled section and provided that electronic course materials are not accessed. Thereafter, no refund will be issued as full access to course content has been granted.

Under certain circumstances, a live class may be cancelled up to 5 days in advance of the scheduled start date. Students will be provided with rescheduling options which could include access to self-study materials when live courses are not available. If rescheduling efforts are not successful, a refund for the cancelled course section may be issued and access suspended provided that the section content has not been accessed.

No Shows are students who never attend a live/live online class and do not access any portion of the course software/electronic materials.

For **Atlanta Intensive and Final Review students***, a full tuition refund (minus all applicable savings) will be issued to students who withdraw on or before the 2nd class of the first scheduled part. Thereafter, no refund will be issued as full access to course content has been granted.

For **SkillMaster Workshops**: A full refund will be issued to students who withdraw at least 10 business days before the scheduled workshop. Thereafter, no refund will be issued.

(*Applicable in all states except those noted below.)

The following cancellation policy is applicable for students in Alabama, Arkansas, District of Columbia, Kansas, Kentucky, Louisiana, Nebraska, Nevada, New Hampshire, New Mexico, Oklahoma, West Virginia:

If cancellation occurs within 3 business days of registration, all monies paid by the student will be refunded even if classes have already started.

A full tuition refund (minus all applicable savings and fees) will be issued to students who withdraw on or before the 5th business day after the start date of the first scheduled section; thereafter, students are entitled to a prorated refund (minus all applicable savings and fees) for the unused portion through 60% of the part taken (75% in Arkansas and DC).

For example, the refund for a candidate who withdraws after completing 12 hours (3 sessions) of Audit classes will be calculated as follows:

- Amount Paid $1131.00
- Amount to be Prorated $1131.00
- 8 Hours Cancelled / 20 Hours Scheduled × $1131.00 = $452.00 (Amount Refunded)

Residents are not required to submit written notification of withdrawal.

New Hampshire Students: Any buyer may cancel this transaction by submitting written notification of withdrawal any time prior to midnight of the third business day after the date of this transaction.

Oklahoma Students: Becker Professional Education is licensed by Oklahoma Board of Private Vocational Schools, 700 N. Classen Blvd. #250, Oklahoma City, OK, 73118.

Classroom Locations: University of Oklahoma, 307 West Brooks, Room 200, Norman, OK, 73019; Oklahoma Christian University, 2501 E Memorial Rd., Edmond, OK, 73136; and Oklahoma State University, 108 Gunderson Hall, Stillwater, OK, 74078.

Holder in Due Course Rule: Any holder of this consumer credit contract is subject to all claims and defenses which the debtor could assert against the seller of goods and services obtained pursuant hereto or with the proceeds hereof. Recovery hereunder by the debtor shall not exceed that paid by the debtor. (This Federal TradeCom Regulation became in effect 5/14/75.)

Becker Professional Education is licensed by Oklahoma Board of Private Vocational Schools, 700 N. Classen Blvd. #250, Oklahoma City, OK 73118.

Tennessee Students: At a minimum, refunds are calculated as follows:

Date of Withdrawal During:	Percent Refund of Tuition (Less Administrative Fee)
First day of scheduled classes	100%
Balance of week 1	90%
Week 2	75%
Weeks 3 and 4	25%
Weeks 5–8	0%

Refunds are to be prorated as of last day of actual attendance, notification is not required. All monies paid by an applicant will be refunded if requested within three days after signing an enrollment agreement and making an initial payment.

NON-REFUNDABLE ITEMS: Charges for Flashcards, Supplemental Multiple-Choice Questions, 0% APR* Financing Processing Fee and the Becker Promise material license fee are non-refundable.

*Annual Percentage Rating

Attendance:

CPA Exam Review Courses—Live Classroom Non-F1 Students

Attendance is defined as a student physically attending a live classroom on the enrolled/registered dates and times. BPE tracks attendance through rosters at live classes for students who selected and enrolled in this format. Classroom coordinators or student assistants are responsible for collecting attendance information. The faculty member supervises the attendance process at each class.

The purpose of BPE's CPA Exam review course is to prepare students for the CPA Exam. BPE does not issue grades, degrees, licenses or diplomas at course completion. A student may request a live course completion certificate by calling Becker's customer service at 800-868-3900. CPA live course completion certificates are offered for each section of the course (Audit, Business, Financial and Regulation). A student must attend a minimum of 50% of the live lectures for each section to receive the course completion certificate for that section. The student must complete any classes not attended live by viewing the corresponding lecture content (which is similar in length and content as the Live Course) using Becker's e-learning platform. The student must demonstrate completion of the relevant e-learning lectures by providing the Performance Summary report. Upon confirmation that the student has completed 100% of the lectures with at least 50% of the lectures in the live classroom, the student will receive the course completion certificate.

Students who are tardy or depart early must notify the instructor who will note on the attendance sheet with "T" for tardy (arriving 20 or more minutes late) and/or "ED" at early departure (leaving 20 or more minutes before the end of class). All students are required to sign in upon arrival at the class. Note that receiving a "T" or "ED" means that student may not count that class toward the live attendance requirement to receive a completion certificate.

No Shows are students who never attend a live/live online class and do not access any portion of the course software/electronic materials.

CPA Exam Review Courses—LiveOnline (LiveOnline courses are not I-20 eligible)

Attendance is defined as a student logging in to a LiveOnline webcast on the enrolled/registered dates and times. BPE tracks attendance using the webinar platform's built-in tracking of when registered students log in and log off. LiveOnline webcast registration and attendance tracking are the responsibility of the U.S. Accounting Operations team.

The purpose of BPE's CPA Exam review course is to prepare students for the CPA Exam. BPE does not issue grades, degrees, licenses or diplomas at course completion. A student may request a LiveOnline course completion certificate by calling Becker's customer service at 800-868-3900. CPA LiveOnline course completion certificates are offered for each section of the course (Audit, Business, Financial and Regulation). A student must attend a minimum of 50% of the LiveOnline lectures for each section to receive the course completion certificate for that section. The student must complete any classes not attended via webcast by viewing the corresponding lecture content using Becker's e-learning platform. The student must demonstrate completion of the relevant e-learning lectures by providing the Performance Summary report. Upon confirmation that the student has completed 100% of the lectures with at least 50% of the lectures via LiveOnline webcast, the student will receive the course completion certificate. Students who arrive more than 20 minutes late or leave more than 20 minutes early may not count that class toward the LiveOnline attendance requirement.

No Shows are students who never attend a live/live online class and do not access any portion of the course software/electronic materials.

Course Overview: To review Becker's full live course overview, catalog and policies applicable to live course enrollment, please visit https://www.becker.com/content/dam/bpe/cpa/live/pdf/cpa_exam_review_course_catalog_4-6-18.pdf

Auditing: This course includes 18 hours of live instruction* and prepares students to pass the Auditing and Attestation section of the CPA Exam.

Business: This course includes 18 hours of live instruction* and prepares students to pass the Business Environment and Concepts section of the CPA Exam.

Financial: This course includes 30 hours of live instruction* and prepares students to pass the Financial Accounting and Reporting section of the CPA Exam.

Regulation: This course includes 24 hours of live instruction* and prepares students to pass the Regulation section of the CPA Exam.

*Hours of instruction represent allotted schedule time for live classes. Actual pre-recorded lecture hours may vary.

Exclusion of Warranties: YOU EXPRESSLY ASSUME ALL RISK FOR USE OF THE MATERIALS. YOU AGREE THAT THE MATERIALS ARE PROVIDED TO YOU "AS IS" AND "AS AVAILABLE" AND THAT BECKER MAKES NO WARRANTIES, EXPRESS OR IMPLIED, WITH RESPECT TO THE MATERIALS, THEIR MERCHANTABILITY OR FITNESS FOR A PARTICULAR PURPOSE AND NO WARRANTY OF NONINFRINGEMENT OF THIRD PARTIES' RIGHTS. NO DEALER, AGENT OR EMPLOYEE OF BECKER IS AUTHORIZED TO PROVIDE ANY SUCH WARRANTY TO YOU. BECAUSE SOME JURISDICTIONS DO NOT ALLOW THE EXCLUSION OF IMPLIED WARRANTIES, THE ABOVE EXCLUSION OF IMPLIED WARRANTIES MAY NOT APPLY TO YOU. BECKER DOES NOT WARRANT OR GUARANTEE THAT YOU WILL PASS ANY EXAMINATION.

Exclusion of Damages: UNDER NO CIRCUMSTANCES AND UNDER NO LEGAL THEORY, TORT, CONTRACT, OR OTHERWISE, SHALL BECKER OR ITS DIRECTORS, OFFICERS, EMPLOYEES, OR AGENTS BE LIABLE TO YOU OR ANY OTHER PERSON FOR ANY CONSEQUENTIAL, INCIDENTAL, INDIRECT, PUNITIVE, EXEMPLARY OR SPECIAL DAMAGES OF ANY CHARACTER, INCLUDING, WITHOUT LIMITATION, DAMAGES FOR LOSS OF GOODWILL, WORK STOPPAGE, COMPUTER FAILURE OR MALFUNCTION OR ANY AND ALL OTHER DAMAGES OR LOSSES, OR FOR ANY DAMAGES IN EXCESS OF BECKER'S LIST PRICE FOR A LICENSE TO THE MATERIALS, EVEN IF BECKER SHALL HAVE BEEN INFORMED OF THE POSSIBILITY OF SUCH DAMAGES, OR FOR ANY CLAIM BY ANY OTHER PARTY. Some jurisdictions do not allow the limitation or exclusion of liability for incidental or consequential damages, so the above limitation or exclusion may not apply to you.

Indemnification and Remedies: You agree to indemnify and hold Becker and its employees, representatives, agents, attorneys, affiliates, directors, officers, members, managers, and shareholders harmless from and against any and all claims, demands, losses, damages, penalties, costs or expenses (including reasonable attorneys' and expert witnesses' fees and costs) of any kind or nature, arising from or relating to any violation, breach, or nonfulfillment by you of any provision of this license. If you are obligated to provide indemnification pursuant to this provision, Becker may, in its sole and absolute discretion, control the disposition of any indemnified action at your sole cost and expense. Without limiting the foregoing, you may not settle, compromise, or in any other manner dispose of any indemnified action without the consent of Becker. If you breach any material term of this license, Becker shall be entitled to equitable relief by way of temporary and permanent injunction without the need for a bond and such other and further relief as any court with jurisdiction may deem just and proper.

Confidentiality: The Materials are considered confidential and proprietary to Becker. You shall keep the Materials confidential and you shall not publish or disclose the Materials to any third party without the prior written consent of Becker.

Use of Your Data: You understand that you will be providing personal information if you register for the Program and that the following will occur: (a) once you have registered, logged in, and activated your account, you will be asked to provide information about yourself as part of the registration process, or as part of your continued use of the Materials. You agree that any registration information you give to Becker will be used and stored by Becker. By using the Materials, you hereby consent to Becker retaining your personal information for purposes of the Program and for future purposes in marketing to you regarding other Becker Products.

Waiver of Liability: You hereby waive any claims, causes of action, and damages, and agree to hold harmless and indemnify Becker and its affiliates, officers, agents, and employees from any claim, suit, or action arising from or related to your use of the Materials, the use and storing of any of your information by Becker, or violation of these terms, including any liability or expense arising from claims, losses, damages, suits, judgments, litigation costs, and attorneys' fees.

SUBJECT TO THE OVERALL PROVISION ABOVE, YOU EXPRESSLY UNDERSTAND AND AGREE THAT BECKER, ITS PARENT CORPORATION, SUBSIDIARIES AND AFFILIATES, AND THE OFFICERS, AGENTS, AND EMPLOYEES OF THOSE ENTITIES, SHALL NOT BE LIABLE TO YOU FOR ANY LOSS OR DAMAGE THAT MAY BE INCURRED BY YOU, INCLUDING BUT NOT LIMITED TO LOSS OR DAMAGE AS A RESULT OF BECKER USING OR STORING YOUR INFORMATION WITH YOUR PROFESSOR OR COLLEGE/UNIVERSITY.

THE LIMITATIONS ON BECKER'S LIABILITY TO YOU IN THE PARAGRAPHS ABOVE SHALL APPLY WHETHER OR NOT BECKER HAS BEEN ADVISED OF, OR SHOULD HAVE BEEN AWARE OF, THE POSSIBILITY OF ANY SUCH LOSSES ARISING.

Severability of Terms: If any term or provision of this license is held invalid or unenforceable by a court of competent jurisdiction, such invalidity shall not affect the validity or operation of any other term or provision and such invalid term or provision shall be deemed to be severed from the license. This Agreement may only be modified by written agreement signed by both parties.

Governing Law: This Agreement shall be governed and construed according to the laws of the State of Illinois, United States of America, excepting that State's conflicts of laws rules. The parties agree that the jurisdiction and venue of any dispute subject to litigation is proper in any state or federal court in Chicago, Illinois, USA. The parties hereby agree to waive application of the UN Convention on the Sale of Goods. If the State of Illinois adopts the current proposed Uniform Computer Information Transactions Act (UCITA, formerly proposed Article 2B to the Uniform Commercial Code), or a version of the proposed UCITA, that part of the laws shall not apply to any transaction under this Agreement.

NOTICE TO STUDENTS: ACCET COMPLAINT PROCEDURE

This institution is recognized by the Accrediting Council for Continuing Education & Training (ACCET) as meeting and maintaining certain standards of quality. It is the mutual goal of ACCET and the institution to ensure that educational training programs of quality are provided. When problems arise, students should make every attempt to find a fair and reasonable solution through the institution's internal complaint procedure, which is required of ACCET accredited institutions and frequently requires the submission of a written complaint. Refer to the institution's written complaint procedure which is published in the institution's catalog or otherwise available from the institution, upon request. Note that ACCET will process complaints which involve ACCET standards and policies and, therefore, are within the scope of the accrediting agency.

In the event that a student has exercised the institution's formal student complaint procedure, and the problem(s) have not been resolved, the student has the right and is encouraged to take the following steps:

1. Complaints should be submitted in writing and mailed, or emailed to the ACCET office. Complaints received by phone will be documented, but the complainant will be requested to submit the complaint in writing.

2. The letter of complaint must contain the following:

   a. Name and location of the ACCET institution;

   b. A detailed description of the alleged problem(s);

   c. The approximate date(s) that the problem(s) occurred;

   d. The names and titles/positions of all individual(s) involved in the problem(s), including faculty, staff, and/or other students;

   e. What was previously done to resolve the complaint, along with evidence demonstrating that the institution's complaint procedure was followed prior to contacting ACCET;

   f. The name, email address, telephone number, and mailing address of the complainant. If the complainant specifically requests that anonymity be maintained, ACCET will not reveal his or her name to the institution involved; and

   g. The status of the complainant with the institution (e.g., current student, former student, etc.).

3. In addition to the letter of complaint, copies of any relevant supporting documentation should be forwarded to ACCET (e.g., student's enrollment agreement, syllabus or course outline, correspondence between the student and the institution).

4. **SEND TO:**

   ACCET
   CHAIR, COMPLAINT REVIEW COMMITTEE
   1722 N Street, NW
   Washington, DC 20036
   Telephone: (202) 955-1113
   Fax: (202) 955-1118 or (202) 955-5306
   Email: complaints@accet.org
   Website: accet.org

Note: Complainants will receive an acknowledgement of receipt within 15 days.

Business

final review sections

Business Section I | *Corporate Governance*

A   Corporate Governance

Business Section II | *Economic Concepts and Analysis*

A   Economic and Business Cycles
B   Market Influences on Business
C   Financial Risk Management

Business Section III | *Financial Management*

A   Capital Structure
B   Working Capital
C   Financial Valuation Methods
D   Financial Decision Models

Business Section IV | *Information Technology*

A   Information Technology (IT) Governance
B   Role of Information Technology in Business
C   Information Security/Availability
D   Processing Integrity
E   Systems Development and Maintenance

Business Section V | *Operations Management*

A   Performance Management
B   Cost Accounting
C   Process Management
D   Budgeting and Analysis
E   Forecasting and Projection

Introduction

Final Review is a condensed review that reinforces your understanding of the most heavily tested concepts on the CPA Exam. It is designed to help focus your study time during those final days between your Becker CPA Exam Review course and your exam date.

This Book

Becker's Final Review is arranged based on the AICPA's blueprints. The blueprints outline the technical content to be tested on each of the four parts of the CPA Exam. The blueprints can be found in the back sections of Becker's main CPA textbooks.

The Software

The Final Review software uses an interactive eBook (IEB) format. Watch the introduction video in the Final Review software for a tour of the IEB features.

We recommend progressing through this course in the following order:

- Review the IEB content, including the video introduction to each topic and the lecture audio associated with each page of the IEB.
- Work the embedded multiple-choice questions for each topic as you progress through the content.
- Work the related multiple-choice questions in the question bank for each topic. There are links from the IEB to the question bank.
- Once you have completed all of the IEB sections, topics, and multiple-choice questions, do the practice Simulations in the software.

Becker Customer and Academic Support

The Becker Customer and Academic Support area is your source for course updates, supplemental materials, and academic support. Just click on Customer and Academic Support under CPA Resources at:

> http://www.becker.com/cpa-review.html

You can access customer service and technical support from Customer and Academic Support or by calling 1-877-CPA-EXAM (outside the U.S. +1-630-472-2213).

I | Corporate Governance

A Corporate Governance

1 Rights, Duties, Responsibilities, and Authority of the Board of Directors and Officers

1.1 Board of Directors

Among the specific duties of directors are the election, removal, and supervision of officers; adoption, amendment, and repeal of bylaws; setting management compensation; initiating fundamental changes to the corporation's structure; and declaration of distributions to owners. Another critical role of the board is to manage any potential conflict of interest that may exist between the shareholders (principal) and senior management (agent). Directors are fiduciaries of the corporation and must always act in the best interests of the corporation.

1.2 Officers

Officers are corporate agents. Officers are fiduciaries of the corporation and must act in the best interests of the corporation. Officers may serve on the board of directors and are not required to be shareholders.

2 Sarbanes-Oxley Act of 2002

The financial reporting issues associated with corporate governance generally relate to the provisions of the Sarbanes-Oxley Act of 2002 (also known as SOX). SOX has numerous provisions for expanded disclosures and specific representations by management that are described in the first two major titles.

2.1 Title III—Corporate Responsibility

- Public companies (also known as issuers) must have an audit committee.

- The audit committee comprises board members who are independent of the company other than their membership on the board of directors. To be independent, an audit committee member cannot be a paid consultant or advisor.

- The external auditor reports to the audit committee.

- The chief executive officer (CEO) and the chief financial officer (CFO) are required to sign off on published reports and represent that the report:

  - was reviewed by each party.

  - does not contain untrue statements or material omissions.

  - contains financial statements that present fairly in all material respects the financial condition and results of operations of the issuer.

- The CEO and CFO are required to represent that they are responsible for internal controls and that the controls are designed to ensure that all material information has been made available to the auditors, and that controls have been evaluated for effectiveness.

- The CEO and CFO must represent whether there have been any significant changes to internal control.

- If the CEO or CFO falsify information about the financial statements, potential penalties include repaying the issuer any bonuses that are equity based or repaying any gains that were realized on the sale of the issuer's stock.

2.2   Title IV—Enhanced Financial Disclosures

- Management must include the following enhanced disclosures in its periodic reports.

  - Material correcting adjustments identified by the auditor should be reflected in the financial statements.

  - Disclosure of all material off-balance sheet transactions.

  - Conformity of pro forma financial statements to certain requirements (no untrue statements or omitted material information; reconciled with GAAP financial statements).

  - The use of special purpose entities (SPEs).

- Disclose any parties that have a direct or indirect ownership of more than 10 percent of any class of most equity securities.

- Management must assess the organization's internal controls and make disclosure of that assessment.

- An issuer must disclose whether or not its senior officers have adopted a code of ethics (conduct). If not adopted, the issuer must explain the reasons.

- Audit committees should have a financial expert.

  - The financial expert is an individual who has expertise developed through education or experience as an auditor or finance officer for an organization of similar complexity.

  - The financial expert must be disclosed.

2.3   Title VIII—Corporate and Criminal Fraud Accountability

- An individual who alters, destroys, conceals, or makes false entries in any record or document with the intent to impede, obstruct, or influence an investigation will be fined, imprisoned not more than 20 years, or both.

- Auditors of issuers should retain all audit and review workpapers for a period of seven years from the end of the fiscal period in which the audit or review was conducted. Failure to do so will result in a fine, imprisonment for not more than 10 years, or both.

- The statute of limitations for securities fraud is no later than the earlier of two years after the discovery of the facts constituting the violation or five years after the violation.

- An employee who lawfully provides evidence of fraud may not be discharged, demoted, suspended, threatened, harassed, or in any other manner discriminated against for providing such information.

- An individual who knowingly executes, or attempts to execute, securities fraud will be fined, imprisoned not more than 25 years, or both.

2.4 Title IX—White-Collar Crime Penalty Enhancements

- An individual who attempts or conspires to commit any white-collar offense will be subject to the penalties as predetermined by the United States Sentencing Commission.

- When an issuer files a periodic report with the SEC that contains financial statements, it must include the following written statements (signatures):

  - The report fully complies with the Securities Exchange Act of 1934.

  - The information contained in the report fairly presents, in all material respects, the financial condition and operating results of the issuer.

  - The above written statements must be signed by the chief executive officer and chief financial officer (or their equivalent) of the issuer, who bear full responsibility for these written statements.

- When a party of the issuer certifies a financial report and/or its contents, knowing that it does not satisfy all three requirements above, he or she will be subject to fines or imprisonment.

2.5 Title XI—Corporate Fraud Accountability

- An individual who alters the integrity of, destroys, or conceals a document used in connection with an official proceeding shall be fined and/or subject to not more than a 20-year prison term.

- As part of cease-and-desist proceedings, the SEC may issue an order that prohibits a person from serving as an officer or director of an issuer, in the event the SEC determines that the person has violated securities rules/regulations and is unfit to continue to serve the issuer in that capacity.

- An individual who knowingly retaliates against a person who provides truthful information to the SEC in connection with a possible federal offense shall be fined or imprisoned for not more than 10 years.

Which of the following is true regarding a financial expert serving on the audit committee of an issuer that is complying with the Sarbanes-Oxley Act of 2002?

1. The audit committee member may qualify for recognition as a financial expert using most any combination of education and experience auditing or preparing financial reports.

2. An audit committee member must have been a member of the board of directors for five years before serving as a financial expert.

3. An audit committee member qualifying as a financial expert must have adequate technical training and experience as an auditor.

4. Disclosure of the financial expert is made at the election of the audit committee.

? Related Questions

For related questions, go to the online question bank:

➤ FR-00781

➤ FR-00788

3 Internal Control

The Committee of Sponsoring Organizations (COSO) issued *Internal Control—Integrated Framework* (the Framework) to assist organizations in developing comprehensive assessments of internal control effectiveness. COSO's framework is widely regarded as an appropriate and comprehensive basis to document the assessment of internal controls over financial reporting.

3.1 COSO Framework Objectives

There are three categories of objectives built within the framework:

1. **Operating Objectives:** These pertain to the effectiveness and efficiency of an entity's operations.

2. **Reporting Objectives:** These relate to the reliability, timeliness, and transparency of an entity's external and internal financial and nonfinancial reporting.

3. **Compliance Objectives:** These are developed to ensure the entity is adhering to existing laws and regulations.

3.2 COSO Framework

The COSO framework comprises five integrated components that logically begin with the tone at the top and conclude with monitoring the effectiveness of internal controls. There are 17 principles that support these 5 components. The mnemonic "**CRIME**" is used to remember these 5 components.

3.2.1   Control Environment

- Referred to as the "tone at the top."
- Ethics, board oversight, commitment to employee competencies, and organizational structure are the foundational principles that define this component.

3.2.2   Risk Assessment

- Identification and analysis of risks related to the entity's objectives is performed under the risk assessment component.
- Organizational objectives, risk and fraud identification, and assessing changes that impact internal control are principles of this component.

3.2.3   Information and Communication

- This principle includes capturing and processing information.
- Financial reporting and internal control information as well as internal and external communication are supporting principles of the information and communication component.

3.2.4   Monitoring

- Monitoring the effectiveness of internal control is the goal of the monitoring component.
- Monitoring by way of ongoing and separate evaluations and reporting findings (deficiencies) are the related principles.

3.2.5   (Existing) Control Activities

- The policies and procedures that respond to the risk assessment are the subject of the control activities component.
- Principles of (existing) control activities include selecting and developing control activities, developing technological controls, and deploying policies and procedures.

3.3   COSO Cube

The three-dimensional COSO cube demonstrates that there is a direct relationship between an entity's three framework objectives, its five integrated internal control components, and the organizational structure of the entity.

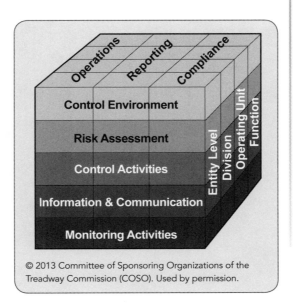

© 2013 Committee of Sponsoring Organizations of the Treadway Commission (COSO). Used by permission.

3.4   Effective (Ineffective) Internal Control— COSO

- The framework defines an effective internal control system as one that provides reasonable assurance that the entity's objectives will be achieved. The framework general requirements include:

  - Five components and 17 principles that are relevant are to be both present and functioning.

  - All five components operating together as an integrated system are a means to reduce the risk to an acceptable level that the entity will not achieve its objectives.

- In order to be considered an effective system of internal control, senior management and the board must achieve reasonable assurance (meet specific requirements) that the entity:

  - understands when its operations are managed effectively and efficiently.

  - complies with applicable rules, regulations, and external standards.

  - prepares financial reports that conform to the entity's reporting objectives and all applicable rules, regulations, and standards.

- When a major deficiency is identified pertaining to the presence and functioning of a component or a relevant principle, or if the components do not operate together in an integrated manner, the entity has an ineffective internal control system under the COSO framework.

Question 3-1   FR-00784

The Committee of Sponsoring Organizations' (COSO) *Internal Control—Integrated Framework* includes five distinct components that include all the following, *except*:

1. Control Environment
2. Risk Assessment
3. Risk Response
4. Control Activities

? Related Questions

For related questions, go to the online question bank:

➤ FR-00783

➤ FR-00785

➤ FR-00789

4 Enterprise Risk Management

In 2004, COSO issued *Enterprise Risk Management (ERM)—Integrated Framework* ("the framework") to assist organizations in developing a comprehensive response to risk management. In recognition of the changing complexity of risk, the emergence of new risks, and the enhanced awareness of risk management by both boards and executive oversight bodies, COSO published *Enterprise Risk Management—Integrating With Strategy and Performance* in 2017. The intent of ERM is to allow management to effectively deal with uncertainty, evaluate risk acceptance, and build value. The underlying premise of ERM is that every entity exists to provide value for stakeholders and that all entities face risk in the pursuit of value for its stakeholders. According to COSO, "Risk is the possibility that events will occur and affect the achievement of strategy and business objectives."

4.1 Themes

The ERM framework includes the following themes.

- ERM is defined by COSO as the *culture*, *capabilities*, and *practices*, *integrated with strategy-setting and performance*, that organizations rely on to *manage risk* in creating, preserving, and realizing *value*.

- Management decisions will impact the development of value including its *creation, preservation, erosion*, and *realization*.

- Mission vision and core values define what an entity strives to be and how it wants to conduct business.

- Core values correlate with culture.

- Mission and vision correlate with strategy and business objectives.

- Risk appetite represents the types and amounts of risk, on a broad level, that an organization is willing to accept in pursuit of value.

- ERM seeks to align risk appetite and strategy.

- Application of ERM is intended to provide management with a reasonable expectation of success with:

  - Enhancement of risk response decisions

  - Identification and management of multiple and cross-enterprise risks

  - Seizing opportunities

  - Improving the deployment of capital

4.2 Objectives

ERM evaluates risk within the context of strategy and business objectives.

4.3 Components

The components of ERM follow in logical sequence using the mnemonic **GO PRO** and are supported by principles memorized as **DOVES SOAR VAPIR SIR TIP**.

4.3.1 **G**overnance and Culture

- Defines **D**esired culture
- Exercises board **O**versight
- Demonstrates commitment to core **V**alues
- Attracts, develops, and retains capable individuals (**E**mployees)
- Establishes operating **S**tructure

4.3.2 Strategy and **O**bjective-Setting

- Evaluates alternative **S**trategies
- Formulates business **O**bjectives
- **A**nalyzes business context
- Defines **R**isk appetite

4.3.3 **P**erformance

- Develops portfolio **V**iew
- **A**ssesses severity of risk (likelihood and impact)
- **P**rioritizes risk
- **I**dentifies risks (events)
- Implements risk **R**esponses (accept, pursue, reduce, share, or avoid)

4.3.4 **R**eview and Revision

- Assesses **S**ubstantial change
- Pursues **I**mprovement in Enterprise Risk Management
- **R**eviews risk and performance

4.3.5 Information, Communications, and Reporting (**O**ngoing)

- Leverages information and **T**echnology
- Communicates risk **I**nformation
- Reports on risk culture and **P**erformance

4.4   Limitations

Although ERM is an outstanding tool, its limitations include being subject to human judgment, evaluations made in error, and management override.

Question 4-1   FR-00786

Using COSO's *Enterprise Risk Management—Integrated Framework* as a basis for dealing with uncertainty while seeking profit and growth, an organization would:

1. Avoid all risk
2. Develop strategy in a manner that aligns with management's risk appetite
3. Only set entity-wide strategic goals
4. Eliminate uncertainty

? Related Questions

For related questions, go to the online question bank:

➤ FR-00787

Task-Based Simulations

Task-Based Simulation: Written Communication

The Chairman of the Board of Directors is worried about the upcoming audit. Specifically, he is concerned about how he will prove to the auditors that the Board of Directors has fulfilled its oversight function in accordance with the COSO Internal Control–Integrated Framework. As the Chief Financial Officer, draft a memo to the Chairman describing what the auditors might look for in regards to the following board attributes:

- Operates independently
- Monitors risk
- Retains financial reporting expertise
- Oversees audit activities

Type your communication in the response area below.

REMINDER: Your response will be graded for technical content and writing skills. Technical content will be evaluated for information that is helpful to the intended audience and clearly relevant to the issue. Writing skills will be evaluated for development, organization, and the appropriate expression of ideas in professional correspondence. Use an appropriate business format with a clear introduction, body, and conclusion. Do not convey information in the form of a table, bullet-point list, or other abbreviated presentation.

Memorandum

To: Chairman, Board of Directors
Re: Board Oversight

Explanation

The purpose of this memo is to identify and explain the kinds of activities that will enable the auditors to conclude that the Board of Directors is fulfilling its oversight function in accordance with the COSO Internal Control—Integrated Framework.

One of the characteristics of an effective board is the ability of each member to provide independent advice to our company. You may recall, annually our company requires each board member to disclose in writing any personal relationships and material direct or indirect financial transactions with our company. In addition to this, we have a process in place where the Vice President of the board reviews these disclosures and evidences his review via signature on the certification statement. Before any vote is taken, the VP verbally reminds board members to vote independently and, if applicable, has the power to ask board members to recuse themselves from the vote in the event that they are not entirely independent on the issue at hand. Although our bylaws document the responsibilities of the Vice President, the board minutes document the actions of the board and VP, consistent with the policy defined in the bylaws. Rest assured that the auditors will review both of these documents and find the evidence to support a conclusion on board oversight.

We also have a separate nominating committee that identifies and screens potential board members. Evidence that the nominating committee has performed their duties includes a review of background checks performed as well as the written recommendations made by this committee.

Another attribute that the auditors will assess is the board's ability to monitor risk. One of the most powerful ways to demonstrate effective board oversight is to establish an empowered audit committee with the authority and responsibility to meet privately with internal and external auditors and respond directly to significant audit findings. Even staffing the audit committee with knowledgeable financial professionals such as CPA's provides additional comfort to auditors that the board has the capacity to understand the gravity of the issues put before them. Although the auditors have both the charter and by-laws to support the creation and empowerment of the audit committee, their selection and retention provides further support that the audit committee is actually performing the responsibilities assigned to it.

Further proof of effective oversight can be obtained by reviewing the certification statements made by the audit committee, which attest to review activities performed and decisions made. In addition, the board minutes document the adoption of new accounting policies and procedures. And lastly, the auditors can examine whistle-blower logs to determine how complaints were handled and the timeliness of the board response.

As you can see, we have a number of mechanisms already in place that will objectively demonstrate the effectiveness of our board. The board does an excellent job and you will be very well prepared to speak to these issues with our auditor.

Feel free to contact me should need anything further regarding this matter.

II Economic Concepts and Analysis

Notes

1 Business Cycles

1.1 Components of the Business Cycle

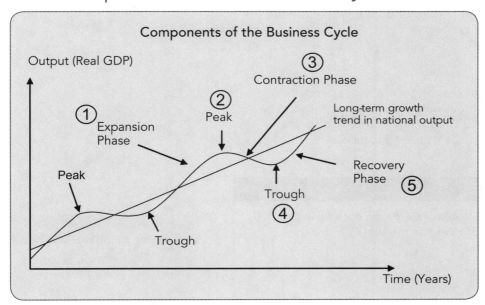

Components of the Business Cycle

Output (Real GDP)

③ Contraction Phase

② Peak

Long-term growth
trend in national output

① Expansion Phase

Recovery Phase ⑤

Peak

Trough ④

Trough

Time (Years)

1.2 Nominal vs. Real GDP

■ Nominal GDP (unadjusted) measures the value of all final goods and services in current prices.

■ Real GDP measures the value of all final goods and services in constant prices, adjusted for changes in the price level (inflation).

$$\text{Real GDP} = \frac{\text{Nominal GDP}}{\text{GDP Deflator}} \times 100$$

1.3 Economic Indicators

■ Leading indicators tend to predict economic activity. Orders for goods would represent a leading indicator.

■ Lagging indicators follow economic activity. Consumer price index for services would be a lagging indicator.

■ Coincident indicators change at generally the same time as the whole economy. Industrial production (GDP) would represent a coincident indicator.

1.4   Aggregate Demand and Supply Curves

- The aggregate demand (AD) curve indicates the maximum quantity of all goods and services that households, businesses, and government are willing and able to purchase at any given price level.

- The aggregate supply (AS) curve indicates the maximum quantity of all goods and services that producers are willing and able to produce at any given price level.

- While changes in the price level will impact the aggregate demand or supply along the AD and AS curves, there are other factors beyond the price level which may cause a shift (inward or outward) in either the AD and/or AS curves (see discussed below).

1.5   Multiplier Effect

When an increase in consumer, business, or government spending generates a multiplied increase in the level of economic activity, this is referred to as the multiplier effect. The change in real GDP, or the multiplier, is calculated as $1 / (1 - MPC)$, where MPC represents the marginal propensity to consume.

Question 1-1   FR-00137

Suppose that in a given year, the nominal GDP of a country is $10,000 billion and the GDP deflator is 125. What is the real GDP for the country?

   1. $12,500 billion.

   2. $10,000 billion.

   3. $8,000 billion.

   4. $80 billion.

?   Related Questions

For related questions, go to the online question bank:

➤   FR-00177

➤   FR-00187

➤   FR-00235

2 Economic Measures/Indicators

2.1 Gross Domestic Product (GDP)

GDP is the measure of the output and performance of a nation's economy. It includes all final goods and services produced by resources within a country, regardless of what country owns the resources (emphasis is on the word "domestic").

2.1.1 The Expenditure Approach (GICE)

- **G**overnment Purchases
- Gross Domestic **I**nvestment
- Personal **C**onsumption
- Net **E**xports

2.1.2 The Income Approach (I PIRATED)

- **I**ncome of Proprietors
- **P**rofits of Corporations
- **I**nterest (net)
- **R**ental Income
- **A**djustments for Net Foreign Income and Miscellaneous Items
- **T**axes
- **E**mployee Compensation
- **D**epreciation

2.2 Other Measures of National Income

2.2.1 Gross National Product (GNP)

GNP is the measure of the market value of all final goods and services produced by residents of a country, regardless of whether or not the resident produces the goods or services domestically or abroad. Emphasis is on the word "national."

2.2.2 Net National Product (NNP)

$$NNP = GNP - Depreciation$$

2.2.3 National Income (NI)

$$NI = NNP - Indirect\ business\ taxes$$

    Business Final Review   **II**   **A-3**

2.2.4 Personal Income (PI)

Income received by households and noncorporate businesses

2.2.5 Disposable Income (DI)

$$DI = PI - \text{Personal taxes}$$

2.3 Measuring Unemployment

2.3.1 The Unemployment Rate

$$\text{Unemployment rate} = \frac{\text{Number of unemployed}}{\text{Total labor force}} \times 100$$

2.3.2 The Labor Force

The total labor force equals all individuals 16 years of age and older who are either working or actively seeking work.

2.3.3 Types of Unemployment

- **Frictional Unemployment:** Normal unemployment due to turnover, etc.
- **Structural Unemployment:** The jobs available do not match skills.
- **Seasonal Unemployment:** Results from seasonal change in labor demand.
- **Cyclical Unemployment:** Results from a decline in real GDP during contraction or recession.
- **Natural Rate of Unemployment:** Frictional unemployment + Structural unemployment + Seasonal unemployment.

2.3.4 The Phillips Curve

The Phillips curve demonstrates the inverse relationship between the rate of inflation and unemployment. When unemployment is high (very low), inflation tends to be low (high).

2.4 Inflation, Deflation, and the Consumer Price Index

2.4.1 Inflation

Sustained increase in general prices of goods and services.

2.4.2 Deflation

Sustained decrease in general prices of goods and services.

2.4.3 The Consumer Price Index (CPI)

Measures the overall cost of a basket of goods and services purchased by an average household during a given period of time. The GDP deflator measures the changes in prices of all new domestically produced final goods and services in an economy.

$$CPI = \frac{\text{Current cost of market basket}}{\text{Base year cost of market basket}} \times 100$$

2.4.4 Inflation Rate

$$\text{Inflation rate} = \frac{CPI_{\text{this period}} - CPI_{\text{last period}}}{CPI_{\text{last period}}} \times 100$$

2.4.5 Producer Price Index (PPI)

Measures the overall cost of a basket of goods and services typically purchased by businesses.

2.4.6 Demand-Pull Inflation

Caused by increases in aggregate demand (i.e., due to an increase in wealth), whereas cost-push inflation is caused by reductions in short-run aggregate supply (i.e., due to a rise in oil prices).

2.5 Budget Deficits and Surpluses

A government incurs a budget surplus when its revenues exceed its spending (costs) during a year. Conversely, a government has a budget deficit when it spends more than it receives (primarily in taxes) during the year. A budget deficit is financed usually by government borrowing.

2.5.1 Cyclical Budget Deficit

Results from temporarily low economic activity.

2.5.2 Structural Budget Deficit

Results from a structural imbalance between government spending and revenue.

2.6 Interest Rates

- **Nominal Interest Rate:** This is the amount of interest paid or earned measured in current dollars. Nominal interest rates and inflation naturally move together.

- **Real Interest Rate:** This is the nominal interest rate less the inflation rate.

2.7   Money (Supply) Definitions

- **M1:** Includes coins, currency, checkable deposits, and traveler's checks.
- **M2:** Includes M1 plus CDs less than $100,000, money market deposits at banks, mutual fund accounts, and savings accounts.
- **M3:** M2 plus time CDs of deposit of $100,000 or more.

2.8   Effect of Government Fiscal Policy on the National Economy

- **Expansionary Fiscal Policy:** Money Supply ↑, Real GDP ↑, Unemployment ↓
- **Contractionary Fiscal Policy:** Money Supply ↓, Real GDP ↓, Unemployment ↑
- Fiscal policy can affect firm investment through its effect on interest rates.

2.9   The Federal Reserve and Monetary Policy

The Fed controls the money supply through:

- **Open Market Operations:** Buying and selling government securities.
- **Changes in the Discount Rate:** Interest rate for short-term loans to member banks.
- **Changes in the Required Reserve Ratio:** Fraction of bank deposits held in reserve.

2.10   The Money Supply and Interest Rates

2.10.1   Increase in Money Supply = Decrease in Interest Rates

- Purchasing government securities;
- Lowering the discount rate; or
- Lowering the required reserve ratio.

2.10.2   Decrease in Money Supply = Increase in Interest Rates

- Selling government securities;
- Increasing the discount rate; or
- Increasing the required reserve ratio.

2.11   Inflation, Recessions, and Changes in the Money Supply

2.11.1   Stimulate Economy During a Recession

Increase the money supply, causing interest rates to fall, real GDP to rise, the unemployment rate to decline, and the price level to rise.

2.11.2 Control of Inflation

Decrease the money supply, causing interest rates to rise, real GDP to fall, the unemployment rate to rise, and the price level to fall.

Question 2-1   FR-00157

Consider an economy with 1,000 people, 600 who hold jobs, 200 who are looking for work, 100 who have given up looking for a job, and 100 who are under the age of 16 or retired. The total labor force and unemployment rate, respectively, are:

1. 800, 25%
2. 900, 33%
3. 900, 22%
4. 800, 37.5%

Question 2-2   FR-00207

Which of the following is an example of expansionary fiscal policy?

1. A decrease in the required reserve ratio.
2. An increase in the discount rate.
3. A decrease in government spending.
4. A decrease in taxes.

? Related Questions

For related questions, go to the online question bank:

➤ FR-00127
➤ FR-00147
➤ FR-00167
➤ FR-00197
➤ FR-00217
➤ FR-00246
➤ FR-00255

1 Demand

1.1 Fundamental Law of Demand

Fundamental law of demand states that the price of a product/service and the quantity demanded of that product/service are inversely related due to the:

- **Substitution Effect:** Consumers tend to purchase more (less) of a good when its price falls (rises) in relation to the price of other goods.

- **Income Effect:** When prices are lowered (income kept constant), consumers will purchase more of the lowered-price products.

1.2 Factors That Shift Aggregate Demand

Factors that shift aggregate demand include changes in:

- Consumer wealth
- Real interest rates
- Expectations regarding future economic outlook
- Exchange rates
- Government spending
- Consumer taxes (personal income taxes)

1.3 Factors That Shift the Demand Curve

Factors that shift demand curves include changes in:

- Wealth
- Price of related goods (substitutes and complements)
- Consumer income
- Consumer tastes or product preferences
- Consumer expectations
- Number of buyers served by the market

Question 1-1   FR-00259

A reduction in the personal income tax will tend to cause:

    1. Unemployment and real GDP to fall.

    2. Unemployment and real GDP to rise.

    3. Unemployment to rise and real GDP to fall.

    4. Unemployment to fall and real GDP to rise.

? Related Questions

For related questions, go to the online question bank:

➤ FR-00227

2 Supply

2.1 Fundamental Law of Supply

Fundamental law of supply states that price and quantity supplied are positively related.

2.2 Factors That Shift Short-Run Aggregate Supply

Factors that shift short-run aggregate supply include:

- Changes in input (resource) prices
- Supply shocks

2.3 Factors That Shift the Supply Curve

Factors that shift supply curves include changes in:

- Price expectations of supplying firm
- Product costs
- Price or demand of other goods
- Subsidies or taxes
- Product technology

3 Market Equilibrium

3.1 Equilibrium Price and Output

A market's equilibrium price and output (quantity) is the point on the graph (next page) where the supply and demand curves intersect. This is also called the market's clearing price.

3.2 Changes in Equilibrium

- When the demand curve shifts right, equilibrium price and quantity will increase.
- When the demand curve shifts left, equilibrium price and quantity will fall.
- When the supply curve shifts right, equilibrium price will fall and equilibrium quantity will increase (i.e., more of the good will be produced and sold at a lower price).
- When the supply curve shifts left, equilibrium price will increase and equilibrium quantity will fall.

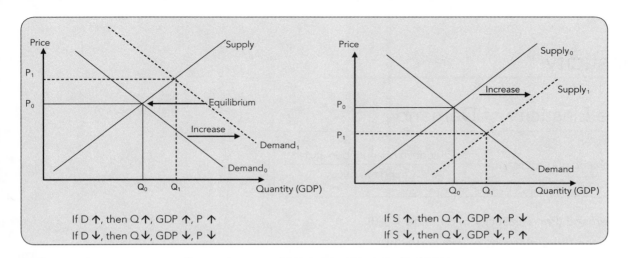

If D ↑, then Q ↑, GDP ↑, P ↑
If D ↓, then Q ↓, GDP ↓, P ↓

If S ↑, then Q ↑, GDP ↑, P ↓
If S ↓, then Q ↓, GDP ↓, P ↑

Question 3-1   FR-00128

Which of the following events would lead to an increase in the equilibrium price of a good and a decrease in the equilibrium quantity?

1. A decrease in consumer income.

2. An increase in production costs.

3. An increase in the price of a substitute good.

4. A decrease in the price of a complementary good.

Question 3-2   FR-00241

When the supply curve shifts to the left:

1. Equilibrium price and quantity will rise.

2. Equilibrium price and quantity will fall.

3. Equilibrium price will rise and equilibrium quantity will fall.

4. Equilibrium price will fall and equilibrium quantity will rise.

4 Elasticity

4.1   Price Elasticity of Demand

$$\text{Price elasticity of demand} = \frac{\% \text{ Change in quantity demanded}}{\% \text{ Change in price}}$$

- Inelastic demand (Price elasticity of demand < 1.0)
- Elastic demand (Price elasticity of demand > 1.0)
- Unit elastic demand (Price elasticity of demand = 1.0)

4.2   Price Elasticity of Supply

$$\text{Price elasticity of supply} = \frac{\% \text{ Change in quantity supplied}}{\% \text{ Change in price}}$$

- Inelastic supply (Price elasticity of supply < 1.0)
- Elastic supply (Price elasticity of supply > 1.0)
- Unit elastic supply (Price elasticity of supply = 1.0)

4.3   Cross Elasticity and Income Elasticity of Demand

4.3.1   Cross Elasticity

Per the formula below, a positive coefficient indicates substitute goods, whereas a negative coefficient indicates complement goods.

$$\text{Cross elasticity of demand (supply)} = \frac{\% \text{ Change in number of units of X demanded (supplied)}}{\% \text{ Change in price of Y}}$$

4.3.2   Income Elasticity of Demand

Per the formula below, if the income elasticity of demand is positive then the good is a normal good, whereas if the income elasticity of demand is negative then the good is an inferior good.

$$\text{Income elasticity of demand (supply)} = \frac{\% \text{ Change in number of units of X demanded (supplied)}}{\% \text{ Change in income}}$$

Question 4-1   FR-00138

When the price of shrimp rises from \$5 per pound to \$6 per pound, the quantity demanded of shrimp falls from 100 pounds to 90 pounds. What is the price elasticity of demand for shrimp?

1. 0.10
2. 2.00
3. 0.50
4. 0.70

? Related Questions

For related questions, go to the online question bank:

➤ FR-00148

➤ FR-00251

5 Production Costs in the Short (Long) Run

5.1 Short-Run

- Production costs in short run are both fixed and variable.
- Cost functions:
  - Average fixed cost = FC/Q
  - Average variable cost = VC/Q
  - Average total cost = TC/Q
  - Marginal cost = $\Delta TC / \Delta Q$

5.2 Long-Run

All production costs in the long-run are variable with the long-run average total cost (LRATC) curve being U-shaped.

6 Market Structures

Market structure refers to the type of market within which firms operate.

6.1 Perfect Competition

- A large number of firms
- Very little product differentiation
- No barriers to entry
- Firms are price takers

6.2   Monopolistic Competition

- A relatively large number of firms
- Differentiated products sold by the firms in the market
- Few barriers to entry
- Firm has control over quantity produced with price set by the market

6.3   Oligopoly

- Very few firms selling differentiated products
- Fairly significant barriers to entry
- Firms are interdependent (i.e., the actions of one firm affect the actions of other firms)
- Firms face kinked demand curves (match price cuts; ignore price increases).

6.4   Monopoly

- A single firm in a market
- Significant barriers to entry
- No substitute products for the good
- The ability of a firm to set output and prices

Question 6-1   FR-00158

In a perfectly competitive market, firms are likely to:

1. Devote significant resources to promote product differentiation.
2. Face significant barriers to market entry.
3. Match price cuts by competitors but ignore price increases.
4. None of the answer choices are correct.

? Related Questions

For related questions, go to the online question bank:

- ➤ FR-00168
- ➤ FR-00252
- ➤ FR-00256
- ➤ FR-00260
- ➤ FR-00263

7 Developing and Implementing Strategy

7.1 Factors That Influence Strategy (SWOT)

■ Internal factors (**s**trengths and **w**eaknesses)

■ External factors (**o**pportunities and **t**hreats)

7.2 Porter's Five Forces Affecting Competition and Firm Profitability

■ Barriers to market entry

■ Market competitiveness

■ Existence of substitute products

■ Bargaining power of customers

■ Bargaining power of suppliers

7.3 Types of Competitive Strategies

7.3.1 Cost Leadership Strategies

■ Broad range of buyers

■ Narrow range (niche) of buyers

■ Successful in markets where buyers have large bargaining power and price competition exists

7.3.2 Differentiation Strategies

■ Broad range of buyers

■ Narrow range (niche) of buyers

■ Successful in markets where customers see value in individual products

7.3.3 Best Cost Strategies

■ Combines cost leadership and differentiation strategies

■ Successful when generic products are not considered acceptable but customers are sensitive to value

7.3.4 Focus/Niche Strategies

■ Focus is on satisfying a particular customer segment (niche)

■ Successful when niche is large enough so that firm can generate a profit

Question 7-1 FR-00247

Sportin' Dude Water Craft markets a range of personal watercraft for use in the ocean, rivers, or lakes. The company has been quite successful, but it has noted a decline in sales since the discovery of the dreaded Bombay virus, an ear infection caused by microbes that have been discovered this year in rivers and lakes throughout North America. When Sportin' Dude prepares its strategic plan, it will likely identify the discovery of the microbe as a:

1. Strength.
2. Weakness.
3. Opportunity.
4. Threat.

Question 7-2 FR-00228

Rivington Corporation is reviewing its competitive strategy. It has been following a combined cost leadership/differentiation/vertical integration strategy for its general retail merchandise division, but that strategy has not been working too well and the company has been losing market share to national competitors. Which of the following statements is/are more than likely correct with respect to competitive strategies?

I. Cost leadership strategies typically focus on building market share and matching the prices of rival firms. A possible reason for the lack of success of Rivington's cost leadership strategy is that it has an outmoded warehousing and distribution system.

II. Differentiation strategies attempt to gain competitive advantage by creating the perception that products are superior to those of competitors. A possible reason for the lack of success of Rivington's differentiation strategy is that it implemented its strategy by advertising its "everyday low prices."

III. Vertical integration strategies attempt to control an entire supply chain. A possible reason for the lack of success of Rivington's strategy is that it had not acquired any of the companies in its supply chain.

1. I and II only are correct.
2. I and III only are correct.
3. I only is correct.
4. I, II, and III are correct.

? Related Questions

For related questions, go to the online question bank:

➤ FR-00188

8 Value Chain Analysis

8.1 Part of Strategic Planning

Value chain analysis helps a company meet or exceed customer expectations. Types of value chain analysis include:

- Internal costs analysis
- Internal differentiation analysis
- Vertical linkage analysis

8.2 Steps in Value Chain Analysis

1. Identify the value chain activities.

2. Identify the cost drivers associated with each activity.

3. Develop competitive advantage by either:
   - reducing cost; or
   - adding value.

Question 8-1   FR-00178

Canal Corporation is considering value chain analysis. Which of the following statements is/are correct with respect to value chain analysis?

I.   Value chain analysis is a tool used by companies to assess the perceived value of a company by potential stockholders.

II. Value chain analysis starts with an identification of cost drivers and ends with the development of means of obtaining competitive advantage.

III. Types of value chain analysis are internal cost analysis, internal differentiation analysis, and vertical linkage analysis, all of which examine internal costs to determine perceived value and competitive advantage.

   1. I, II, and III are correct.

   2. II only is correct.

   3. I and III only are correct.

   4. None of the listed choices are correct.

---

9 Supply Chain Management

9.1 Supply Chain Operations Reference (SCOR) Model

- Plan
- Source
- Make
- Deliver

9.2 Benefits of Supply Chain Management

- Reduced inventory, warehousing, and packaging costs
- Reduction of delivery and transportation costs
- Improved service and delivery times
- Management and integration of suppliers
- Cross-docking (minimization of handling and storage costs)

Task-Based Simulations

Task-Based Simulation: Written Communication

The owner of a private school is trying to increase its revenues to meet rising costs. Capacity is limited and you have been asked to comment on the ways in which revenue can be increased.

Prepare a memorandum to the owner describing why pure price increases may result in increased revenue.

Type your communication in the response area below.

REMINDER: Your response will be graded for technical content and writing skills. Technical content will be evaluated for information that is helpful to the intended audience and clearly relevant to the issue. Writing skills will be evaluated for development, organization, and the appropriate expression of ideas in professional correspondence. Use an appropriate business format with a clear introduction, body, and conclusion. Do not convey information in the form of a table, bullet-point list, or other abbreviated presentation.

Memorandum

To: Private School Owner
Re: Price Increases

Explanation

Increasing tuition may be a highly effective method of increasing revenue. Although increases in tuition may result in decreased enrollment, if the percentage increase in revenue exceeds the percentage decrease in enrollment, total revenue will increase.

The inelasticity of demand (the idea that demand will remain relatively unchanged in responses to changes in price) is generally equated with essential items for survival like water, food, or even fuel. However, the quality of education of our children has a strong perceived value to the families already enrolled. Clearly, the families you serve have elected to use your school rather than rely on public schools, which are available free of charge.

As you review your strategy for the coming year, recognize you are electing to differentiate yourself from the competition as a premier choice in education that is worth the price, not as a cost leader underselling other options.

Revenue can increase based on tuition increases, but you will need to insure that the demand for your school's service is differentiated from the competition and remains an alternative that cannot be easily duplicated.

Let me know if you need further assistance on this issue.

1 Risk Definitions—Exposures to Loss

1.1 Interest Rate (Yield) Risk

Losses in underlying asset value or increases in underlying liability value as a result of changes in market interest rates.

1.2 Market Risk

Losses in trading value of asset or liability in markets. Market risk is nondiversifiable risk.

1.3 Credit Risk

Inability to secure debt financing in a timely and affordable manner.

1.4 Default Risk

The possibility that a debtor may not repay the principal or interest due on their debt obligation on a timely basis.

1.5 Liquidity Risk

The investor desires to sell a security but cannot do so on a timely basis or without material price concessions.

Question 1-1   FR-00269

Arbor Corporation is evaluating its working capital financing needs. Management is concerned about increasing interest rates and has elected to fund its working capital needs with an equity loan from Harbor National Bank collateralized by land. The Arbor Corporation's decision is most likely designed to minimize:

1. Interest rate risk.
2. Market risk.
3. Credit risk.
4. Default risk.

? Related Questions

For related questions, go to the online question bank:

➤ FR-00266

2 Computation of Return

2.1 Stated Interest Rate

The rate of interest charged before adjustments for compounding or market factors.

2.2 Effective Interest Rate

The actual finance charge associated with a borrowing after reducing the loan proceeds for charges and fees.

2.3 Simple Interest Rate

The amount of interest paid on the original principal without including compounding. The formula is: $SI = P_0(i)(n)$

2.4 Compound Interest

The amount of interest earnings or expense that is based on the original principal plus unpaid interest earnings or expense. The formula is:
$FV_n = P_0(1 + i)^n$

2.5 Required Rate of Return

Start with the risk-free rate and add the market risk premium, inflation premium, liquidity risk premium, and default risk premium.

Question 2-1   FR-00826

The required rate of return consists of which of the following?

1. Simple interest rate + compounding premium + market risk premium + inflation risk premium + default risk premium.

2. Effective interest rate + market risk premium + default risk premium.

3. Compound interest rate + default risk premium + market risk premium + inflation risk premium.

4. Risk-free rate + market risk premium + inflation premium + liquidity risk premium + default risk premium.

---

3 Financial Decisions Using Probability and Expected Value

3.1 Probability

Probability represents a chance (expressed as a percentage) that an event will occur, with a zero (0 percent) assigned when there is no chance an event will occur and a one (100 percent) assigned if there is complete certainty that an event will occur. For example, the probability of selecting an M from the 26 letters of the alphabet is 1 in 26 or 1/26.

3.2 Expected Value

Expected value is the weighted average of the probability assigned to each expected outcome of occurrence. For example, if the probability of selling 5,000 cars is 20 percent and the probability of selling 4,000 cars is 80 percent, the expected value is 4,200 cars [(80% × 4,000) + (20% × 5,000)].

4 Circumstances Creating Exchange Rate Fluctuations

Exchange rate fluctuations are generally caused by two factors.

4.1 Trade Factors

- Inflation rates
- Income levels
- Government controls

4.2 Financial Factors

- Interest rates
- Capital flows

Question 4-1 FR-00236

An international firm based in the United States is forecasting the impact of various factors on its trade in foreign markets. Each of the following factors would serve to improve the exchange rate of the United States dollar relative to foreign currencies, except:

1. Foreign inflation.

2. Declining domestic income.

3. Low foreign interest rates.

4. Increased foreign capital investment.

---

5 Risk Exposures Implied by Exchange Rate Fluctuations

5.1 Transaction Exposure

Dealing in foreign currencies exposes the parties involved to potential economic loss or gain upon settlement of a transaction in a foreign currency. (Note: This is either a purchase transaction resulting in a payable or a sales transaction resulting in a receivable.)

5.2 Economic Exposure

Exposure to economic risks related to exchange rate fluctuations pertains to the possibility that the value of cash flows could fluctuate up or down as a result of changes in the exchange rate.

The following diagram summarizes the relationship.

Assume: at $time_0 \rightarrow \$1 = €1$

	Receive € (Net inflows)	Paying € (Net outflows)
If U.S. \$ appreciates to \$0.75 = €1→	**1.** Loss	**2.** Gain
If U.S. \$ depreciates to \$1.25 = €1 →	**3.** Gain	**4.** Loss

Example

1. Company A has a €100 receivable. The U.S. \$ appreciates from \$1 = €1 to \$0.75 = €1. Originally, once this €100 was received, it could be converted to \$100 at the initial exchange rate. But, when the U.S. \$ appreciates, the same €100 receivable can only be converted to \$75 (loss).

2. If Company A had a payable of €100, originally it cost \$100. But when the U.S. \$ appreciates, the same €100 payable can be satisfied with \$75 (gain).

3. If Company A has a €100 receivable and the U.S. \$ depreciates from \$1 = €1 to \$1.25 = €1, once the €100 is received, it can be converted to €100 = \$125 (gain).

4. If Company A has a €100 payable and the U.S. \$ depreciates, to satisfy the €100 payable, it requires \$125 instead of \$100 (loss).

5.3 Translation Exposure

Translation exposure is the potential that the consolidation of the financial statements of domestic parents with foreign subsidiaries will result in changes in account balances and income as a result of exchange rate fluctuations. Translation exposure increases as the degree of involvement by the parent with international subsidiaries increases. This exposure is also affected by the stability of a foreign currency versus the parent currency, with a stable (unstable) foreign currency decreasing (increasing) translation risk. Translation exposure is also known as accounting exposure.

Question 5-1   FR-00242

Shore Co. records its transactions in U.S. dollars. A sale of goods resulted in a receivable denominated in Japanese yen, and a purchase of goods resulted in a payable denominated in euros. Shore recorded a foreign exchange gain on collection of the receivable and an exchange loss on settlement of the payable. The exchange rates are expressed as so many units of foreign currency to one dollar. Did the number of foreign currency units exchangeable for a dollar increase or decrease between the contract and settlement dates?

	Yen exchangeable for $1	Euros exchangeable for $1
1.	Increase	Increase
2.	Decrease	Decrease
3.	Decrease	Increase
4.	Increase	Decrease

Question 5-2   FR-00198

Hickman International is based in the United States, but it conducts significant business in Canada. The company's exposure to economic risks of exchange rate fluctuation include:

1. The potential that accounts receivable denominated in Canadian dollars may be exchanged for fewer United States dollars at the settlement date than on the date of origination.

2. The potential that net sales in Canadian markets (inflows) are denominated in a devalued currency that is less valuable than the United States dollar, thereby reducing the present value of the company.

3. The potential that the remeasurement of subsidiary financial statements denominated in Canadian dollars may produce a foreign exchange loss.

4. The potential that translated financial statements might reflect a reduction in comprehensive income.

6 Hedging to Mitigate Exchange Rate Transaction Exposure

Hedging is a financial risk management technique in which an entity, that is attempting to mitigate the risk fluctuations in exposure, acquires a financial instrument that behaves in the opposite manner from the hedged item. There are several hedging transactions that can be used by an entity to mitigate transaction exposure from both an accounts payable and accounts receivable application basis.

6.1 Futures Hedge

A futures hedge entitles the holder to either purchase or sell a number of currency units for a negotiated price on a stated date. Futures hedges are used for smaller amounts.

6.2 Forward Hedge

A forward hedge is similar to a futures hedge, but the owner of the contract is entitled to buy or sell volumes of currency at a point in time. Forward contracts identify groups of transactions for larger amounts.

6.3 Money Market Hedge

Money market hedges use foreign money markets to meet future cash flow needs and mitigate exchange rate risks by investment in financial institutions of the foreign economy. Money market hedges may be executed with either excess cash discounted and invested in the foreign economy or through simultaneous borrowing and reinvesting in the foreign economy.

6.4 Currency Option Hedge

Currency option hedges use the same principles as forward hedge contracts and money market hedge transactions, except the owner has the option (and not the obligation) to execute the hedge transaction. The acquisition of an option requires payment of consideration (a premium). The owner of the option must consider the cost of the premium as part of determining the value of exercising the option.

6.5 Long-Term Forward Contract

A long-term forward contract works like any other forward contract but is used to stabilize transaction exposure over long periods. An entity may use long-term forward contracts to hedge long-term purchase contracts.

6.6 Currency Swap

A currency swap can be used to mitigate transaction exposure for longer term transactions. For example, two firms may enter into a currency swap whereby the firms agree to swap their currencies received at a future date for a negotiated exchange rate.

Question 6-1   FR-00208

Siaggas International is a United States corporation with substantial dealings in Europe. The company is hedging the amounts it owes on individual accounts payable denominated in euros. The financial instrument most likely used by the company would be:

1. Futures contracts to buy the specific number of euros to settle the debt at the spot rate at the time the liability was incurred.
2. Futures contracts to sell the specific number of euros to settle the debt at the spot rate at the time the liability was incurred.
3. Forward contracts to buy the monthly requirement of euros to satisfy anticipated accounts payable for the month.
4. Forward contracts to sell the monthly requirement of euros to satisfy anticipated accounts payable for the month.

Related Questions

For related questions, go to the online question bank:

➤ FR-00218

7 Hedging to Mitigate Economic and Translation Exposure

Economic and translation exposure to exchange rate fluctuations involves overall business planning and design which create potential exposures to cash flow (economic) or financial reporting (translation) risks related to exchange rate fluctuation.

7.1 Restructuring

Economic exposure to currency fluctuations can be mitigated by restructuring the sources of income and expense to the consolidated entity. A downside to restructuring is that it is usually more difficult to manage than ordinary hedges.

8 Transfer Pricing

The primary reason for developing transfer pricing arrangements between domestic parents and foreign subsidiaries is to minimize local taxation. Additionally, intercompany cash transfers are often managed through the use of a "leading" transfer policy (subsidiaries with strong cash position) or a "lagging" transfer policy (subsidiaries with weak cash position).

III | Financial Management

1 Factors Affecting Short-Term and Long-Term Financing

1.1 Short-Term Financing

Advantages of short-term financing include increased liquidity, higher profitability, and lower financing costs. Disadvantages of short-term financing are higher interest rate risk and reduced capital availability.

1.2 Long-Term Financing

Advantages of long-term financing are lower interest rate risk and increased capital availability. Disadvantages of long-term financing include reduced profitability, decreased liquidity, and higher financing costs.

2 Methods of Short-Term Financing

2.1 Working Capital Financing

Working capital financing entails current assets being financed with trade accounts payable and accrued liabilities.

2.2 Letter of Credit

A letter of credit is a third-party guarantee (e.g., a bank).

2.3 Line of Credit

A line of credit is a revolving line of short-term borrowing with a financial institution.

Question 2-1   FR-00221

Cash Burn Enterprises is entering a period of intense cash utilization. The company is apprehensive about cash flow timing and ensuring consistent cooperation of its vendors to provide needed supplies. Management would likely use what short-term financing instruments or strategies to meet this challenge:

1. Letter of credit.

2. Line of credit.

3. Subordinated debentures.

4. Working capital financing.

? Related Questions

For related questions, go to the online question bank:

➤ FR-00132

3 Methods of Long-Term Financing

3.1 Leasing Options

3.1.1 Operating Leases

Operating leases are often referred to as "off-balance sheet financing" because there is no balance sheet effect for the lessee (just rent expense recorded on income statement). An operating lease is a pure rental agreement, in which there is no change of ownership.

3.1.2 Capital Leases

Capital leases transfer "substantially all" of the risks and benefits of ownership associated the lease (asset) to the lessee. The lessee records both an asset and liability on the balance sheet, and recognizes both depreciation expense and interest expense on the income statement.

3.2 Debentures and Bonds

Bonds are a form of indebtedness that obligates the borrower to pay an agreed coupon payment (usually semiannually) over a period of years.

3.2.1 Debentures

Debentures are unsecured bonds that are backed by the full faith and credit of the issuer.

3.2.2 Subordinated Debentures

Subordinated debentures are unsecured obligations that rank behind senior fixed-income securities in the event of an issuer liquidation.

3.2.3 Income Bonds

Income bonds are fixed-income securities that pay interest only upon achievement of target income levels.

3.2.4 Mortgage Bonds

Mortgage bonds are long-term loans that are secured by residential or commercial real property.

3.3 Equity Financing

3.3.1 Preferred Stock

Preferred stock is a hybrid security that has similar features to both debt and equity. Preferred shareholders usually receive a fixed dividend payment, and in the event of an issuer liquidation, rank higher than common stockholders in regard to the claim to the issuer's assets. Usually, preferred stockholders do not have voting rights.

3.3.2 Common Stock

Common stock is the basic equity ownership of a corporation. Although common stockholders may receive capital gains (in addition to periodic dividends) when holding the issuer's stock, they have a residual (last) claim to the issuer's assets in the event of a liquidation.

4 Debt Covenants

Creditors use debt covenants in their lending agreements to protect their interests by limiting or prohibiting the action of the debtor that might negatively affect the position of the creditors. Debt covenants can be positive (i.e., the issuer must provide periodic financial statements), negative (i.e., restriction on asset sales), or financial (i.e., minimum interest coverage ratio).

5 Leverage

5.1   Operating Leverage

■ Operating leverage is the degree to which a firm uses fixed operating costs, as opposed to variable operating costs.

■ A firm with significant operating leverage must have sufficient sales revenues to cover high fixed operating costs.

■ Beyond breakeven, a firm with higher fixed costs will retain a higher percentage of additional revenues as operating income.

5.2   Financial Leverage

■ Financial leverage is defined is the degree to which a firm uses debt (as opposed to equity) in its capital structure.

■ A firm with significant financial leverage must have sufficient operating income (EBIT) to cover fixed interest costs.

■ Once the interest costs are covered, additional EBIT goes straight to net income and earnings per share.

Question 5-1   FR-00816

Which of the following statements is true for both operating and financial leverage?

1. Financing the firm with a very high percentage of common stock relative to long-term debt is a technique used to achieve both financial and operating leverage.

2. Investors and firms both use leverage in an attempt to increase profits, although there is no guarantee this will happen.

3. Using a high degree of both types of leverage (financial and operating) is an excellent way to minimize risk.

4. Increasing variable operating expenses results in higher leverage for a manufacturing firm.

---

6 Cost of Capital Computations

6.1   Cost of Long-Term Debt

The after-tax cost of debt is the multiplication of the pretax cost of debt by one minus the tax rate, as follows:

6.1.1   After-Tax Cost of Debt

$$
\begin{aligned}
\text{Cost of debt (after tax)} &= \text{Interest rate} \times (1 - \text{Tax rate}) \\
&= 0.125 \times (1 - 0.30) \\
&= 0.125 \times 0.70 \\
&= 0.0875
\end{aligned}
$$

The terms are defined as follows:

Cost of debt = Before-tax cost of debt (Face amount × Coupon rate) [*Assumed to be 12.5%*]

(1 − Tax rate) = 1 minus tax rate stated as a decimal [*Tax rate assumed to be 30%*]

6.2   Cost of Equity Capital

6.2.1   Cost of Preferred Stock

$$
\begin{aligned}
\text{Cost of preferred stock} &= \text{Preferred stock dividends} / \text{Net proceeds of preferred stock} \\
&= 10 / (100 - 5) \\
&= 10 / 95 \\
&= 0.10526
\end{aligned}
$$

The terms are defined as follows:

Preferred stock dividends = Cash dividends on preferred stock [*Assumed to be $10 per share*]

Net proceeds of preferred stock = Proceeds of preferred stock sale net of fees and costs
[*Assumed to be $100 and $5 per share, respectively*]

A   Capital Structure

6.2.2 Cost of Common Stock—Discounted Cash Flows (DCF) Method

> Cost of common equity = (Expected dividend / Current stock price) + Constant growth rate in dividends
>
> $\qquad$ = (2.15 / 25.25) + 0.075
>
> $\qquad$ = 0.0851 + 0.075
>
> $\qquad$ = 0.1601

The assumed amounts are:

> 16.01% = Cost of common equity
>
> $2.15 = Expected dividend
>
> $25.25 = Current stock price
>
> 7.5% = Constant growth rate in dividends

6.3 Capital Asset Pricing Model (CAPM)

In addition to the DCF method shown above, the cost of retained earnings can be calculated using the capital asset pricing model (CAPM).

6.3.1 CAPM Formula for Cost of Retained Earnings

The CAPM formula may be expressed as:

> Cost of retained earnings = Risk-free rate + Risk premium
>
> $\qquad$ = Risk-free rate of return + $\left(\text{Beta coefficient of stock} \times \text{Market risk premium} \right)$
>
> $\qquad$ = Risk-free rate of return + $\left[\text{Beta coefficient of stock} \times \left(\text{Market rate} - \text{Risk-free rate of return} \right) \right]$
>
> $\qquad$ = 0.05 + [1.2 × (0.14 − 0.05)]
>
> $\qquad$ = 0.158

The assumed amounts are:

> 5% = Risk-free rate of return
>
> 1.2 = Beta coefficient of stock
>
> 9% = Market risk premium (14% − 5%)
>
> 14% = Market rate

6.4 Weighted Average Cost of Capital (WACC)

The weighted average cost of capital is the sum of the weighted percentage of each form of capitalization used by a business. The optimal cost of capital is the combination of debt and equity securities (debt to equity ratio) that produces the lowest weighted average cost of capital.

6.4.1 Formula

$$\text{WACC} = \begin{array}{c}\text{Cost of equity multiplied}\\\text{by the percentage equity}\\\text{in capital structure}\end{array} + \begin{array}{c}\text{Cost of debt multiplied}\\\text{by the percentage debt}\\\text{in capital structure}\end{array}$$

6.4.2 Optimal Cost of Capital

The following graph illustrates the relationship between the weighted average cost of capital and the relationship between the elements of an entity's capitalization (the debt-to-equity ratio).

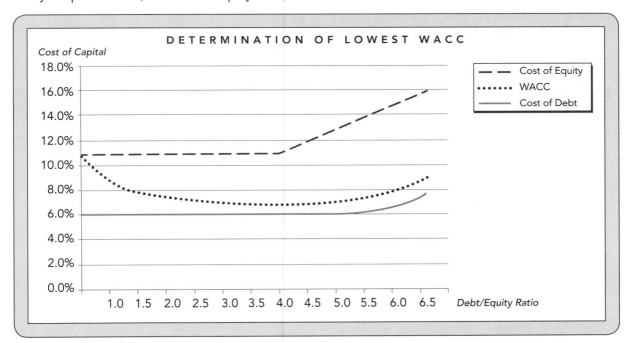

A   Capital Structure

Question 6-1   FR-00131

Gibson Enterprises issued 1,000 of its 8%, $50 par value preferred shares for $52 per share and incurred $2,500 in flotation costs. What was Gibson's cost of equity capital?

1. 8.42%
2. 8.08%
3. 8.00%
4. 7.69%

Question 6-2   FR-00141

SmallCap Corp. is a relatively new company whose limited number of low-cost shares are actively traded on the NASDAQ. The value of the company's shares is fairly volatile and has fluctuated by 25% more than the overall fluctuation of the values of the total exchange. The expected return on the market is 12%. The company has the cash from accumulated earnings necessary for its expansion and currently has the funds in highly liquid, risk-free, federally insured securities yielding 2%. Management has elected to use the capital asset pricing model (CAPM) to compute its cost of capital to assist in evaluating financing alternatives. What is the cost of capital using the CAPM?

1. 2.00%
2. 12.00%
3. 14.50%
4. 10.00%

? Related Questions

For related questions, go to the online question bank:

➤ FR-00151

➤ FR-00201

1 Debt Ratios

1.1 Solvency

Solvency is a measure of security for long-term creditors/investors.

$$\text{Debt-to-equity ratio} = \frac{\text{Total debt}}{\text{Total shareholders' equity}}$$

$$\text{Debt-to-total-assets ratio} = \frac{\text{Total debt}}{\text{Total assets}}$$

2 Working Capital Ratios

2.1 Liquidity

Liquidity measures a firm's short-term ability to meet its current obligations.

$$\text{Current ratio} = \frac{\text{Current assets (Cash + Marketable securities + Receivables + Inventory + Prepaid expenses)}}{\text{Current liabilities}}$$

$$\text{Quick (acid-test) ratio} = \frac{\text{Cash + Marketable securities + Receivables}}{\text{Current liabilities}}$$

3 Cash Management Strategies

Cash management objectives include fee reduction, expediting deposits, and fraud protection.

3.1 Fee Reduction

3.1.1 Compensating Balances

Bank fees are waived when the customer maintains minimum account balances.

3.1.2 Trade Credit

Trade credit maximizes the availability of funding with no (or reduced) charges.

3.1.3 Commercial Paper

Commercial paper is a source of short-term financing by the issuer and an investment of idle cash by the buyer.

3.2 Expedite Deposits

3.2.1 Zero-Balance Account

The zero-balance account maintains a zero balance at all times. Its use reduces the elapsed time for transfers between accounts and maximizes availability of idle cash.

3.2.2 Electronic Fund Transfers (EFTs)

Electronic fund transfers allow for direct deposit of funds.

3.2.3 Lockbox System

With a lockbox system, customers send payments to a PO box or a location accessible by the bank.

3.3 Fraud Protection

Official bank checks (aka depository transfer checks) are designed to insulate the company from fraud and simplify bookkeeping.

Question 3-1   FR-00122

A cash manager trying to increase the availability of cash would likely use any one of the following techniques or banking services, except:

1. Compensating balance arrangements.
2. Zero-balance account arrangements.
3. Electronic funds transfer agreements.
4. Lock box systems.

---

4 Cash Discounts Used in Credit Terms

Different elements of working capital can be used to manage current position.

4.1 Accounts Payable

Cash discounts are frequently offered for early payment of accounts payable or receivable. The terms are stated with the percentage discount available if paid within a discount period along with the full term of the obligation. The term "2/10, net 30" indicates that payment within 10 days will earn a 2 percent discount, but that the full payment is due within 30 days. The cost of discounts not taken can be calculated using the following steps:

1. Compute the number of times the discount-forgone period occurs in a year:

   > Days per year ÷ Days outstanding after discount
   >
   > For terms 2/10, net 30:
   >
   > 360 days per year ÷ (30 days term − 10 days discount) = 360 ÷ 20 = 18

2. Compute the effective interest rate associated with discount forgone:

   > Discount % offered ÷ (100% − Discount % offered)
   >
   > For terms 2/10, net 30:
   >
   > 2% ÷ (100% − 2%) = 0.020408

3. Annualize by multiplying the effective rate by the number of times the discount-forgone period occurs in a year:

   > 0.020408 × 18 times = 36.7%

Question 4-1   FR-00192

Cable Services Corporation offers cash discounts to its customers at terms of 2/12 net 30. Assuming a 360-day year, the maximum annualized interest rate Cable would earn from customers who elect to forgo the discount opportunity and pay at the end of the term would be:

1. 24.0%
2. 36.7%
3. 40.8%
4. 61.2%

---

5 Operating and Cash Conversion Cycles

5.1 Operating Cycle

The length of time from the initial expenditure until the time the cash is collected from customers. The operating cycle is calculated by adding the inventory conversion period (number of days sales in inventory) to the receivables collection period.

5.1.1 Inventory Turnover Ratio

The inventory turnover ratio measures the number of times over an accounting period that inventory is sold.

$$\text{Inventory turnover} = \frac{\text{Cost of goods sold}}{\text{Average inventory balance}}$$

5.1.2 Number of Days Sales in Inventory

The average number of days inventory is held before it is sold.

$$\text{Number of days sales in inventory} = \frac{365}{\text{Inventory turnover}}$$

5.1.3 Receivables Turnover

Receivables turnover measures the number of times receivables are collected over an accounting period (typically one year).

$$\text{Receivable turnover} = \frac{\text{Net credit sales}}{\text{Average receivables}}$$

5.1.4 Receivables Collection Period

The average number of days after a typical credit sale is made until the firm receives payment.

$$\text{Average collection period} = \frac{365}{\text{Receivable turnover}}$$

5.2 Cash Conversion Cycle

The cash conversion cycle, or net operating cycle, adjusts the operating cycle for the time in which vendors are paid by the firm for the initial expenditure. The cash conversion cycle takes the operating cycle and subtracts the payables deferral period.

5.2.1 Accounts Payable Turnover

Accounts payable turnover measures the number of times payables are paid by the firm over an accounting period.

$$\text{Accounts payable turnover} = \frac{\text{Cost of goods sold}}{\text{Average accounts payable}}$$

5.2.2 Accounts Payable Deferral Period

The average number of days a firm takes to pay its vendors for purchases made on credit.

$$\text{Accounts payable deferral period} = \frac{365}{\text{Accounts payable turnover}}$$

Question 5-1   FR-00162

XYZ Corporation had net credit sales of $730,000 for the year ended December 31, Year 3, up over 8% from prior year levels of $675,000. The company has experienced a nearly 15% increase in accounts receivable from $41,000 at December 31, Year 2, to $47,000 at December 31, Year 3. Management wants to know if the average collection for the current year has deteriorated from prior year levels of under 21 days. What is the average collection period in days for the year ended December 31, Year 3?

1. 16.59
2. 22.00
3. 22.86
4. 23.50

? Related Questions

For related questions, go to the online question bank:

➤ FR-00202

6 Accounts Receivable

Accounts receivable can be sold (factored) to expedite cash collections. Factors will typically charge a fee on all receivables purchased, as well as interest on cash given in advance to the seller prior to the factor collecting from the seller's customers.

7 Inventory Management Techniques

Inventory management techniques focus on maintaining the minimum quantities on hand necessary to meet current needs.

7.1 Just-in-Time

A just-in-time inventory system reduces the lag time between inventory arrival and inventory use. It assumes zero defects.

7.2 Economic Order Quantity (EOQ)

Economic order quantity formulates the order size that will minimize both ordering costs and carrying costs.

$$EOQ = \sqrt{\frac{2SO}{C}}$$

The terms are defined as follows:

> EOQ = Economic order quantity
>
> S = Annual sales in units
>
> O = Cost per purchase order (primarily production set-up costs)
>
> C = Carrying cost per unit

Question 7-1

FR-00142

Efficiency Emporiums owns retail outlets exclusively devoted to the marketing and distribution of closet organizers that it purchases wholesale from a supplier. The company will sell 2,500 units in the coming year. The company has estimated that the cost of a purchase order is $1,000, the per unit cost of carrying a unit of product in inventory is $500, and that the stock-out costs associated with inventory is $25,000. What is the optimal inventory order for Efficiency Emporiums?

1. 100
2. 120
3. 208
4. 240

1 Valuation Methods

Traditional financial valuation is based on the formula for the present value of an annuity. The formula is somewhat complex, but is applied in various forms throughout the financial management topic. Alternative valuation methods use variations of the price earnings (P/E) ratio. It is important to understand the valuation formulas, the implied assumptions of the formulas, and the effect of the behavior of financial managers on the evaluation of those assumptions.

2 Calculating the Present Value of an Annuity

2.1 Formula

$$\text{Annuity present value} = C \times (1 - \text{Present value factor} / r)$$
$$= C \times \{(1 - [1 / (1 + r)^t]) / r\}$$

The terms are defined as follows:

C = Cash annuity payment

r = Rate of return

t = Number of years

2.2 Assumptions

Key assumptions include the:

- Recurring amount of the annuity
- Appropriate discount rate
- Duration of the annuity
- Timing of the annuity

3 Perpetuities (Zero Growth Stock)

When a company is expected to pay the same dividend each period, the perpetuity formula can be used to determine the value of the company's stock. The formula (below) implies that the stock price will not increase because the dividend does not increase.

3.1 Per Share Valuation

> Present value of a perpetuity = Stock value per share = $P = D/R$

The terms are defined as follows:

> P = Price
>
> D = Dividend
>
> R = Required return

3.2 Assumptions

Key assumptions include:

- The dividend (and assume it will never change)
- The required return

4 Constant Growth (Dividend Discount Model)

If dividends are assumed to grow at a constant rate, the Gordon (constant) growth model can be used to determine the intrinsic (true) value of the company's stock.

4.1 Per Share Valuation With Assumed Growth

> Stock value per share with assumed growth = $P_t = D_{(t+1)} / (R - G)$

The terms are defined as follows:

> P_t = Current price (price at period "t")
>
> $D_{(t+1)}$ = Dividend one year after period "t"
>
> R = Required return
>
> G = (Sustainable) Growth rate

4.2 Assumptions

Key assumptions include:

- The calculation of dividends one year beyond the year in which you are determining the price.
- A required rate of return.
- A constant dividend growth rate.
- The formula implies that the stock price will grow at the same rate as the dividend, which is not unreasonable, especially for a mature company.

5 Price Multiples

5.1 Price-Earnings (P/E) Ratio

The P/E ratio, once calculated, can be applied to expected earnings (E_1) in order to determine the current stock price. It requires that earnings be greater than zero.

> $$P/E\ Ratio = P_0/E_1$$

The terms are defined as follows:

> P_0 = Price or value today
>
> E_1 = Expected earnings in one year

C Financial Valuation Methods

5.2 PEG Ratio

The PEG ratio is a measure that demonstrates the effect of earnings growth on a company's P/E, assuming a linear relationship between P/E and growth.

$$PEG = \left[(P_0 / E_1) / G\right]$$

$$\text{Value of equity } (P_0) = PEG \times E_1 \times G$$

The terms are defined as follows:

P_0 = Price or value of stock today

E_1 = Expected earnings in one year

G = Growth rate = 100 × Expected growth rate

5.3 Price-to-Sales Ratio

This price multiple can also be used to determine the intrinsic value of stock. The rationale for using this multiple is that sales are less subject to manipulation than earnings and sales can be used to generate a meaningful multiple even when the company's earnings are negative.

$$\text{Value of equity } (P_0) = [P_0 / S_1] \times S_1$$

The terms are defined as follows:

P_0 = Price or stock value today

S_1 = Expected sales in one year

5.4 Price-to-Cash Flow Ratio

The price-to-cash flow ratio is another multiple that can be used to calculate a stock's intrinsic value. This multiple may be preferred over P/E because cash flows are more difficult to manipulate than earnings and empirical evidence indicates that the P/CF multiple is more stable than the P/E ratio.

$$P / CF = P_0 / CF_1$$

$$\text{Value of equity } (P_0) = (P_0 / CF_1) \times CF_1$$

The terms are defined as follows:

> P_0 = Price or stock value today
>
> CF_1 = Expected cash flow in one year

5.5   Price-to-Book Ratio

The price-to-book ratio may be used to value a stock's intrinsic value. Unlike the prior multiples that focus on the income statement or the cash flow statement, the P/B ratio focuses on the balance sheet (common shareholders' equity).

> $$P / B = P_0 / B_0$$
>
> Value of equity $(P_0) = (P_0 / B_0) \times B_0$

The terms are defined as follows:

> P_0 = Price or stock value today
>
> B_0 = Book value of common equity

5.6   Assumptions

Price multiple ratios have similar assumption requirements, which can be influenced by management behaviors, including:

- Future earnings
- Future cash flows
- Future sales
- Future growth rate
- Duration of sales or earnings trends

6   Discounted Cash Flow Analysis (DCF)

Discounted cash flow analysis attempts to determine the intrinsic value of a stock by determining the present value of its expected future cash flows. DCF models used by analysts to perform an absolute valuation on an equity security include the dividend discount model (DDM), the free cash flow to equity (FCFE) model, and the free cash flow to the firm (FCFF) model.

7 Evaluating Assumptions Used in Valuations

Forecasting methods have numerous subjective elements that are subject to behavioral influences. These influences generally include:

7.1 Generalized Rules of Thumb

Generalized rules of thumb distort objective evaluation of evidence.

- Tendency to use stereotyped characterizations
- Use adjustments from presumed baselines
- Use of intuition rather than analysis

7.2 Behavior Biases

- Excessive optimism
- Confirmation bias
- Overconfidence
- Illusion of control

7.3 Effect of Loss Aversion

- Losses are more distracting than gains
- Managers are generally averse to sure losses

Question 7-1   FR-00827

Financial valuation of securities and companies can be accomplished with a number of different models, such as discounted cash flow, Gordon constant growth model, price/earnings multiples, etc. For all of them, varying assumptions are made, some of which are objective and some of which are subjective. Influences on the subjective assumptions can include all of the following except which one?

1. Generalized rules of thumb, which distort objective evaluation of evidence by the tendency to use stereotyped characterizations and adjustments from presumed baselines.

2. Behavioral biases, such as excessive optimism and overconfidence.

3. The effect of loss aversion, meaning managers are generally averse to sure losses.

4. The risk-free rate and volatility of the stock prices are constant over the option's life.

Financial decisions are often influenced by behavioral factors. Which of the following is generally considered most distracting:

1. Overconfidence
2. Business losses
3. Use of available data
4. Excessive optimism

8 Models for Valuing Options

8.1 Valuing Options—Black-Scholes Model

A number of different factors enter into the determination of the value of an option. A commonly used method for option valuation is the Black-Scholes model. The calculation itself is extremely complex and most likely beyond the scope of the CPA Exam.

However, you do need a high-level understanding of the concepts and assumptions that underlie Black-Scholes. Accountants may use this method in valuing stock options when accounting for share-based payments. Option price calculators are widely available, so you do not need to understand the complexity of the actual calculations to apply this method.

8.2 Black-Scholes Model Inputs—Determinants of Option Value

- Current price of the underlying stock (higher price = higher option value)
- Option exercise price
- Risk-free interest rate (higher rate = higher option value)
- Current time until expiration (longer time = higher option value)
- Some measure of risk for the underlying stock (higher risk = higher option value)
- The dividend on the optioned stock (higher dividend = higher option value)

8.3 Assumptions

- Stock prices behave randomly.
- The risk-free rate and volatility of the stock prices are constant over the option's life.
- There are no taxes or transaction costs.

- The stock pays no dividends, although the model can be adapted to dividend-paying stock.

- The options are European-style (exercisable only at maturity).

- An option may or may not have value.

8.4 Limitations of the Black-Scholes Model

Despite its current use, the Black-Scholes model does have several limitations:

- Due to the model's assumptions, results generated from the Black-Scholes model may differ from real prices.

- It assumes instant, cost-less trading, which is unrealistic in today's markets.

- The model tends to underestimate extreme price movements.

- The model is not applicable to pricing American-style options.

1 Tax Effects of Decisions

After-tax cash flows are used in capital budgeting models.

1.1 After-Tax Costs and Benefits

1.1.1 After-Tax Costs

The formula for computing an after-tax cost follows:

> (1.00 − Tax rate)* × Tax-deductible cash expense = After-tax cost (Net cash outflow)
>
> * Complement of tax rate

1.1.2 After-Tax Benefits

The formula for computing an after-tax benefit follows:

> (1.00 − Tax rate)* × Taxable cash receipt = After-tax benefit (Net cash inflow)
>
> * Complement of tax rate

1.2 Depreciation Tax Shield

Even though depreciation does not directly affect cash flows, it does reduce the amount of income tax a company will pay: this effect is called a depreciation tax shield.

1.2.1 Formula

The formula for computing the tax shield follows:

> Tax rate × Depreciation expense = Depreciation tax shield

Question 1-1 FR-00211

PV Corporation (PVC) is evaluating an investment with an annual $150,000 pretax cash inflow for the next five years. The project will require additional working capital of $35,000. The tax rate is 35% and the anticipated additional depreciation for the project is $50,000. The company's hurdle rate is 8% and the related annuity and present value of $1 factors are as follows:

Present value of an annuity at 8% for 5 years	3.9927
Present value of $1 at 8% for 5 years	0.6806

ABC would compute first-year annual after-tax cash flows associated with the program at:

1. 100,000
2. 115,000
3. 130,000
4. 459,160

? Related Questions

For related questions, go to the online question bank:

➤ FR-00121

2 Discounted Cash Flow

Discounted cash flow (DCF) valuation methods (including the net present value and the internal rate of return methods discussed below) are techniques that use time value of money concepts to measure the present value of cash inflows and cash outflows expected from a project.

2.1 Factors

The following elements must be known:

- Dollar amount of initial investment.
- Rate of return desired for the project (discount rate).
- Dollar amount of future cash inflows and outflows (net of related income tax effects).

3 Net Present Value (NPV)

The net present value approach is generally thought to be the best technique to evaluate capital projects.

3.1 Characteristics

Net present value computations are based upon amounts (not percentages). The net present value method displays the net amount by which the present value of cash inflows exceeds (or does not exceed) the invested amount.

3.2 Formula

Discounted cash flows	$XXX
Less: Investment	<XXX>
NPV	XXX

3.3 Conclusions

Positive NPV indicates that the proposed investment exceeds the hurdle (minimum) rate and the investment should be considered. Investments that have a negative NPV should be rejected. A zero NPV indicates the proposed investment is expected to yield the exact hurdle rate of return.

3.4 Capital Rationing and the Profitability Index

3.4.1 Unlimited Capital

Pursue all investment options with a positive NPV.

3.4.2 Limited Capital

Allocate capital to the combination of projects with the maximum NPV.

3.4.3 Profitability Index

A means of ranking projects based on NPV.

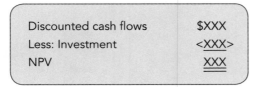

$$\text{Profitability index} = \frac{\text{Present value of net future cash inflow}}{\text{Present value of net initial investment}}$$

The higher this index is, the higher the expected NPV.

Question 3-1 FR-00161

Exeter Corporation has the opportunity to make a $150,000 capital investment that management anticipates will produce a $40,000 after-tax income stream in each of the next five years. The investment will have a 10% salvage value after taxes at the end of year five. The company's tax rate is 25% and the company's hurdle rate is 10%. What is the net present value of this investment given the following present value factors at 10%?

	Present Value of $1.00	Present Value of an Annuity
Year 1	0.909	0.909
Year 2	0.826	1.736
Year 3	0.751	2.487
Year 4	0.683	3.170
Year 5	0.621	3.791

1. ($1,600)
2. $1,600
3. $9,315
4. $10,955

? Related Questions

For related questions, go to the online question bank:

➤ FR-00171
➤ FR-00191

4 Internal Rate of Return (IRR)

4.1 Characteristics

The internal rate of return method computes the percentage rate of return on a specific investment for comparison to a company's target (hurdle) rate of return. The internal rate of return produces a NPV equal to zero.

4.2 Limitations

Internal rate of return computations are less reliable than net present value computations when the investment alternative has variable cash flows. The IRR computation assumes the reinvestment of earnings at the IRR, a rate that may be unrealistic. In the absence of a financial calculator, interpolation and trial and error are required in order to calculate the IRR (unlikely on the exam).

5 Payback Methods

Payback methods may use either discounted or undiscounted approaches. The methods compute the number of years it will take to recoup the original investments.

5.1 Undiscounted Payback

5.1.1 Characteristics

Payback methods are based upon periods of time, not amounts of dollars or percentage returns.

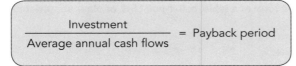

$$\frac{\text{Investment}}{\text{Average annual cash flows}} = \text{Payback period}$$

5.1.2 Objectives and Limitations

The undiscounted payback method ignores profitability and the time value of money.

5.2 Discounted Payback

The discounted payback method is identical to the undiscounted method, except the after-tax cash flows are discounted in the computation for the number of years.

Question 5-1	FR-00181

Inexacta Enterprises wants to compute the payback on a $100,000 capital investment that is projected to produce $23,850 in after-tax cash inflows each year for the next five years and has a 7% salvage value at the end of the fifth year. What is the payback period in years?

1. 3.90
2. 4.19
3. 4.49
4. 5.93

D Financial Decision Models

Task-Based Simulations

Task-Based Simulation: Written Communication

The new staff member at your company is confused about the underlying assumptions of net present value and internal rate of return calculations. As the manager, write a memo to the staff member describing the difference between the two techniques as well as the advantages and disadvantages.

Type your communication in the response area below.

REMINDER: Your response will be graded for technical content and writing skills. Technical content will be evaluated for information that is helpful to the intended audience and clearly relevant to the issue. Writing skills will be evaluated for development, organization, and the appropriate expression of ideas in professional correspondence. Use an appropriate business format with a clear introduction, body, and conclusion. Do not convey information in the form of a table, bullet-point list, or other abbreviated presentation.

Memorandum

To: Staff Member
Re: NPV vs. IRR

Explanation

Net present value and internal rate of return are two techniques that can be used to evaluate investment opportunities. The net present value method is generally considered to be superior to the internal rate of return method. However, each method has its advantages and disadvantages.

Net present value compares the present value of the cash inflows and outflows from an investment decision. Present value is calculated using a discount rate or hurdle rate chosen by management. An investment with a positive net present value should be accepted and an investment with a negative net present value should be rejected. This method provides an estimate of investment return in dollars and assumes that the cash flows from an investment are reinvested at the discount rate used in the analysis.

The net present value method is superior to the internal rate of return method because it is flexible. Net present value can handle uneven cash flows and the discount rate used to calculate present value can be adjusted for risk. Risk adjustments include assigning higher discount rates to higher risk investments and assigning different discount rates to each period of an investment based on relative risk. The limitation of the net present value method is that it does not provide the true rate of return on an investment.

An investment's internal rate of return is the discount rate that equates the present value of the investment's cash inflows and cash outflows. In other words, internal rate of return is the discount rate that yields a net present value of zero. An investment with an internal rate of return in excess of the hurdle rate should be accepted and an investment with an internal rate of return below the hurdle rate should be rejected.

The primary advantage of the internal rate of return method is that it measures return as a percentage that can be compared to the hurdle rate. However, internal rate of return has several limitations. This method assumes that the cash flows from the investment are reinvested at the internal rate of return. This is an unreasonable assumption if the internal rate of return is unrealistically high or low. In addition, internal rate of return is less reliable when investment cash flows are uneven and does not consider the total profitability of an investment.

Because of the relative advantages and disadvantages of these methods, our company generally evaluates potential investments using both methods. If the two methods result in conflicting investment decisions, we use the results of the net present value method to make the final decision.

IV | Information Technology

1 IT Governance

IT governance is a formal structure for how organizations align IT and business strategies. An IT governance framework should align key questions, metrics, and returns to the business.

IT governance is concerned with the strategic alignment between goals and objectives of the business and the utilization of its IT resources to effectively achieve the desired results. According to the IT Governance Institute, there are five areas of focus:

1. Strategic Alignment
2. Value Delivery
3. Resource Management
4. Risk Management
5. Performance Measures

Question 1-1   FR-00125

The CIO at Be The Best Inc. realized that his company needed technology advancements to keep up with the industry. The CIO has suggested developing an IT strategy scorecard, which would include an innovation section to help address this issue. However, he also wants to ensure that the IT strategy scorecard is in alignment with the corporate strategy scorecard. According to the IT Governance Institute, on which of the following area is the CIO focused?

    1. Value Delivery

    2. Resource Management

    3. Risk Management

    4. Performance Measures

---

2 IT Strategy

IT strategies should intersect with the corporate-level, business-level, and functional-level strategies of the corporation.

Business Final Review

3 Principles of Technology-Driven Strategy Development

- Technology is a core input to the development of strategy.

- Due to the speed at which technology changes, strategy development must be a continual process.

- Technology plays an important role in enabling the flow of information in an organization, including information directly relevant to enterprise risk management across strategy setting and the whole organization.

4 Organization of IT Governance Structure

The governance structure must encompass the following aspects: tone at the top, key stakeholders, governance objectives, and IT strategies and oversight.

4.1 Tone at the Top

Selecting technologies to support an organization reflects the:

- entity's approach to risk management;

- types of events affecting the entity;

- entity's overall information technology architecture; and

- degree of centralization of supporting technology.

4.2 Stakeholders or Participants in Business Process Design

Key stakeholders or participants include:

- Management (its most important role is to provide support and encouragement for development projects and to align information systems with corporate strategies).

- Accountants (may be users and should help to determine system requirements; may be on the development team; should take an active role in designing system controls).

- Information Steering Committee (executive level project steering committee).

- Project Development Team (responsible for development as well as technical implementation and user acceptance).

- External Parties (Major customers or suppliers).

4.3 Governance Objectives

The five governance objectives align with the IT Governance Institute's five areas of focus:

1. Strategic Alignment—defining, maintain, and validating the IT value proposition

2. Value Creation—provision by IT of promised benefits to the organization

3. Resource Management—optimization of knowledge and infrastructure

4. Risk Management—risk awareness of senior management and the organization

5. Performance Measurement—tracking and monitoring strategic initiatives, milestones, and/or deliverables throughout projects

---

Question 4-1   FR-00186

Top management's most important role(s) in business process design is:

    1. Determining information needs and system requirements to communicate to system developers.

    2. Providing support and encouragement for IT development projects and aligning information systems with corporate strategies.

    3. Successful design and implementation of the system.

    4. Facilitating the coordination and integration of information systems activities to increase goal congruence and reduce goal conflict.

? Related Questions

For related questions, go to the online question bank:

➤ FR-00757

---

5 Risk Assessment Process

Organizations develop a risk assessment through the following steps:

5.1 Prepare a Business Impact Analysis

Identification of business units, departments, and processes essential to the survival of an entity.

5.2 Identify Information Resources

Identification of hardware, software, systems, services, people, databases, and related resources important to the department.

5.3 Categorize Information Resources by Impact

Identify information resources either as high, medium, or low impact in relation to the effect on day-to-day operations.

5.3.1 High-Impact Resources

The department cannot operate without this resource because it might experience high recovery costs or endure harm in achievement of the organization's mission or maintenance of reputation.

5.3.2 Medium-Impact Resources

The department could work around the loss of this resource for a limited amount of time but might experience some costs of recovery or endure harm in achievement of the organization's mission or maintenance of reputation.

5.3.3 Low-Impact Resources

The department can operate without this resource for an extended period and might endure harm in achievement of the organization's mission or maintenance of reputation.

Question 5-1   FR-00195

Blue Inc. has one data center and cannot operate the day-to-day activities without the data center. The data center is backed up at the end of every month but Blue does not have a disaster recovery plan in place. What is the appropriate impact classification for this information resource?

1. High
2. Medium
3. Low
4. Medium or Low

? Related Questions

For related questions, go to the online question bank:

➤ FR-00146

➤ FR-00165

5.4 Identify and Categorize Risks by Likelihood

Identify and categorize information resource risks or threats either as a high, medium, or low likelihood of occurrence.

5.4.1 High Likelihood

The risk (threat) is highly motivated, and preventive controls in place to mitigate the risk are ineffective.

5.4.2 Medium Likelihood

The risk (threat) is motivated, but preventive controls in place may impede successful exercise of the vulnerability.

5.4.3 Low Likelihood

The risk (threat) lacks motivation, or preventive controls in place will prevent or significantly impede successful exercise of the vulnerability.

5.5 Information Resources, Associated Risks, and Corrective Actions

Align the high-impact information resources with the appropriate risks and indicate the action decision (high, medium, or low action) needed by the team to mitigate each risk.

High action indicates corrective action is needed immediately. Medium action indicates corrective actions will be implemented in a reasonable time frame. Low action indicates no corrective action is needed.

5.6 Recommendations for Mitigating Risks

Document a recommendation or plan for mitigation of each risk for all high- and medium-risk actions associated with high-impact information resources.

1 The Role of Big Data/Data Analytics and Statistics in Supporting Business Decisions

1.1 What Is Big Data?

Big data is a constantly evolving concept in data management and information technology that incorporates four dimensions.

1. Volume (volume of data is large)
2. Velocity (flow of data is continuous)
3. Variety (big data comes from a variety of sources)
4. Veracity (biases must be mined from big data)

1.2 Data Analytics Processes

Three main data analytical processes used with big data include:

1. Descriptive analytics (describing events that have *already* occurred)
2. Predictive analytics (predicting what *could* happen)
3. Prescriptive analytics (using optimization and simulation algorithms to *affect* future decisions)

1.3 Use of Data Analytics

Four top uses of data analytics:

1. Customer analytics
2. Operational analytics
3. Risk and compliance analytics
4. New products and services innovation analytics

Question 1-1   FR-00206

A major investment bank wants to monitor its key risk areas (regulatory, compliance, and technology) in real time with transparency. How can the bank use data analytics to monitor the key risk areas?

1. Use descriptive analytics to examine all journal entries processed for the entire year.
2. Develop a library of indicators to generate different score levels using real-time data analysis tools.
3. Develop a forecasting model to predict what could happen in each area.
4. Use a deal optimization engine to analyze customer demographics and spending patterns.

? Related Questions

For related questions, go to the online question bank:

➤ FR-00222

2   Role of Information Systems in Key Business Processes Within an Entity

Business information systems process detailed data, and provide information for decision making and strategy development. Business information systems allow a business to collect, process, store, transform, and distribute data.

2.1   Management Information Systems (MIS)

MIS provide comprehensive processing and summarizing of data as well as enable organizations to use data as part of strategic planning and tactical execution. MIS often have subsystems called decision support systems and executive information systems.

2.2   Decision Support Systems (DSS)

DSS assist with analytics and presentation of data for specific decisions (e.g., a system that assists sales personnel with bidding of jobs).

2.3   Executive Information Systems (EIS)

EIS summarize data for executive management (e.g., dashboard reporting of key indicators).

2.4   Accounting Information Systems (AIS)

AIS are a type of MIS and may be partly a transaction processing system and partly a knowledge system. A well-designed AIS creates an audit trail for accounting transactions.

Objectives of an organization's AIS include:

- Recording valid transactions
- Properly classifying those transactions
- Recording transactions at their proper value
- Recording transactions in the proper accounting period
- Properly presenting the transactions and related information in the financial statements

2.5   Inventory Management

Inventory management systems track quantities of items and trigger orders when quantities fall below predetermined levels.

2.6   Customer Relationship Management System (CRM)

CRMs provide sales force automation and customer services to manage customer relationships. The objective of a CRM system is to increase customer satisfaction, which can lead to increased revenue and profitability.

2.7   Enterprise Resource Planning Systems (ERP)

ERPs are cross-functional enterprise systems that integrate and automate many business processes and systems working together in the manufacturing, logistics, distribution, accounting, finance, and human resources functions of a business.

2.8   Supply Chain Management Systems (SCM)

SCM is the integration of business processes from the original supplier to the customer and includes purchasing, materials handling, production planning and control, logistics and warehousing, inventory control, and production distribution and delivery. An entity's SCM system may perform some or all of these functions.

Question 2-1   FR-00226

Oily Gulch Drilling Company has designed a system to evaluate drilling sites. The system considers a wide array of geological and geophysical information as well as recent discoveries to determine the likelihood of successful drilling. This system is most likely considered to be a:

  1. Decision support system.

  2. Transaction processing system.

  3. Executive information system.

  4. Management information system.

? Related Questions

For related questions, go to the online question bank:

➤ FR-00136

3 E-Commerce Technologies

The term *e-commerce* (or electronic commerce) is the electronic completion of buying and selling (exchange) transactions. E-commerce can use a private network or the Internet.

3.1   Electronic Funds Transfers

Electronic funds transfer systems are a major form of electronic payment for the banking and retailing industries and are critical to e-commerce (e.g., paying for a book online by using a credit card). EFT security is normally provided through various types of data encryption. A third-party vendor acts as an intermediary between the user company and the banking system.

3.2   Application Service Providers (ASP)

Application service providers supply access to application programs on a rental basis. They allow smaller companies to avoid the extremely high cost of owning and maintaining today's application systems by allowing them to pay only for what is used. The ASPs own and host the software.

3.3 Web Stores

Many smaller companies have stand-alone Web stores that are not integrated with larger accounting systems. In contrast, many larger companies and some smaller companies use integrated ERP systems that integrate all major accounting functions and the Web store into a single software system (called integrated Web stores).

3.4 Dynamic Content

Any content that changes frequently and includes video, audio, and animation. In the context of HTML and the World Wide Web, it refers to website content that constantly or regularly changes based on user interactions, timing, and other parameters.

3.5 Mash-ups

Mash-ups are Web pages that are collages of other Web pages and other information (e.g., Google maps).

3.6 Cloud Computing

Cloud computing involves virtual servers over the Internet. A primary advantage of cloud computing is that it can offer professional management of hardware and software. Cloud computing includes infrastructure-as-a-service, platform-as-a-service, and software-as-a-service. Cloud providers must have sophisticated backup procedures as well as high-level security for customer data.

Question 3-1   FR-00755

Georgia Corporation utilizes an ASP (Application Software Provider) for its Enterprise Resource Planning system. Which of the following statements is/are correct?

I. Georgia's benefits of utilizing an ASP are lower costs, both from a hardware and software standpoint as well as reducing personnel costs and providing greater flexibility.

II. Georgia's disadvantage of utilizing an ASP are higher costs, both from a hardware and software standpoint as well as reducing personnel costs and providing greater flexibility.

III. Georgia's drawbacks of utilizing an ASP are the possible risks to the security and privacy of the organization's data, the financial viability or lack thereof of the ASP, and possible poor support by the ASP.

IV. ASP allows smaller companies, such as Georgia, to avoid the extremely high cost of owning and maintaining today's application systems by allowing them to pay only for what is used.

   1. I, II, III, and IV are correct.

   2. I and IV only are correct.

   3. I, III, and IV only are correct.

   4. IV only is correct.

? Related Questions

For related questions, go to the online question bank:

➤ FR-00185

1 Protection of Information

1.1 Security Policy

The goal of a good information security policy is to require people to protect information. An entity's information security policy can be defined as a document that states how an organization plans to protect its tangible and intangible information assets. The information security policy may include:

- Management instructions indicating a course of action, a guiding principle, or an appropriate procedure.

- High-level statements that provide guidance to workers who must make present or future decisions.

- Generalized requirements that must be written down and communicated to certain groups of people inside, and in some cases outside, the organization.

1.2 Types of Policies

Computer security policies start out at a high level and become more specific.

- Program-level policy
- Program-framework policy
  - Issue-specific policy
  - System-specific policy

Question 1-1   FR-00763

Security policies should seek to secure information that exists in three distinct states, with exception of:

1. Where and how it is stored
2. Where and how it is formatted
3. Where and how it is processed
4. Where and how it is transmitted

? Related Questions

For related questions, go to the online question bank:

➤ FR-00234

2 Development and Management of Security Policies

A three-level model can be used to develop a comprehensive set of security policies:

1. Define Security Objectives (based on system functionality or mission requirements)
2. Operational Security (define the way a specific data operation would remain secure)
3. Policy Implementation (enforced through technical and/or traditional management methods)

3 Policy Support Documents

Documents that support policies include: regulations, standards and baselines, guidelines, and procedures.

4 Logical and Physical Access Controls

4.1 Logical Controls

Logical controls use software and data to monitor and control access to information and computing systems.

4.1.1 User Access

User accounts are the first target of a hacker who has gained access to an organization's network. Diligent care must be used when designing procedures for creating accounts and granting access to information.

4.1.2 Password Management

A password management policy must address the following characteristics:

■ **Password Length**

The longer, the better. It must be greater than seven characters. Most organizations require at least eight characters.

■ **Password Complexity**

Complex passwords feature three of the following four characteristics: uppercase characters, lowercase characters, numeric characters, and ASCII characters (e.g., ! @ # $ % ^ & * or ?).

■ **Password Age**

The NSA (National Security Agency) recommends that passwords should be changed every 90 days. Administrative passwords should be changed more frequently.

■ **Password Reuse**

Although there is no true standard, passwords should not be reused until a significant amount of time has passed. The goal is to prevent users from alternating between their favorite two or three passwords.

■ **Two-Factor Authentication**

This method allows for a second authentication key from a secondary device that is based on the time of log in.

4.1.3 Network and Host-Based Firewalls

■ Default-deny policy (more secure)

■ Default-allow policy (easier)

4.1.4 Access Control Lists

These lists specify which users or system processes are granted access to objects and what operations are allowed on given objects.

4.1.5 Data Encryption

■ Data security is a central issue for information technology. The encryption of data or information attempts to ensure data security by scrambling information to make it unreadable without an access code (key). Encryption methods include:

■ Encryption keys (used to scramble and unscramble the data; the longer, the better; a popular one is 128 bits).

■ Digital certificates (an electronic document that is digitally signed by a trusted party).

■ Digital signatures (a signature in an electronic form to identify the sender and ensure that the message has not been changed).

■ E-signatures (a legally binding, cursive-style imprint of a person's name applied to an electronic document).

■ None of these methods are foolproof; hackers are always trying to find ways around them.

Question 4-1   FR-00761

Which of the following statements is true about encryption keys?

1. The longer the length of the key, the more confusing it is and the less effective it becomes.

2. One of the most popular encryption methods uses a key length of 288 bits.

3. In a brute-force attack, the attacker simply tries to physically break the Web server.

4. By maintaining the private key as a secret, access is limited, but it does not mean the communication is perfect or that hackers are not trying to develop software that would break encryption schemes.

Question 4-2   FR-00196

Landry Company has a distributed computing environment including mainframe computers in Dallas, mid-range UNIX processors in New York City, and numerous PCs connected to its various LANs. Landry has grown somewhat haphazardly over the years and no longer has any written data processing procedures or controls because the only copy of its data processing procedures manual was destroyed in a fire several years previously. Landry should consider implementing which of the following?

I. Securing access to its mainframe computer room and moving its computer room to a convenient area right under its chemical mixing department.

II. Implementing a new password protection scheme. Currently, all employees use their employee numbers as passwords, and all of the software uses the generic access passwords that were originally provided by the software vendor.

III. Implementing a permanent file backup process to utilize the empty space right next to where the mainframe computer room might be moved that could be easily and cheaply converted into a data storage room.

1. II only is correct.
2. II and III only are correct.
3. I and II only are correct.
4. I, II, and III are correct.

? Related Questions

For related questions, go to the online question bank:

➤ FR-00240

4.2   Physical Controls

Physical controls monitor and control the environment of the workplace and computing facilities. Examples include:

- **Segregation of Duties**

  Ensuring that an individual cannot complete a critical task by himself.

- **Monitoring and Control of Access to and From the Facilities**

  Examples include: doors, locks with retina, separating the network and workplace into functional areas, etc. Physical access to computer rooms should be limited to computer operators and other personnel of the IT department. To restrict access to computer rooms, the entity should require special coded IT cards or entry keys.

- **Backup Files**

  Data backups are required for recovery in a disaster scenario and for recovery from processing problems. The company should store copies of key master files and records off-site with copies of files kept on-site stored in fireproof containers or rooms.

- **Uninterrupted Power Supply (UPS)**

  UPS is a device that maintains a continuous supply of electrical power to connected equipment. A UPS, also called a battery backup, can prevent data loss and can protect the integrity of a backup while it is being performed.

- **Program Modification Controls**

  Program modification controls are controls over changes to programs being used in production applications. They are used to prevent changes by unauthorized personnel and to track program changes so there is record of what version of a program is running in production at a given point in time.

- **Malware Detection**

  Malware detection software detects the threat of viruses, worms, and file infectors.

5   General and Application Controls

5.1   General Controls

General controls are designed to make sure an organization's control environment is stable and well-managed. Some of the more important general controls are system development standards, security management controls and change management procedures, as well as software acquisition, development, operations, and maintenance controls.

5.2 Application Controls

Application controls prevent, detect, and correct transaction error and fraud. Application controls are concerned with accuracy, completeness, validity, and authorization of the data captured, entered into the system, processed, stored, transmitted to other systems, and reported.

6 Disaster Recovery/Business Continuity Plans

Disaster recovery consists of plans for continuing operations in the event of destruction of programs, data, and processing capability. Depending on the organization, the disaster recovery plan may be limited to the restoration of IT processing or may extend to restoration of functions in end-user areas (sometimes called a business continuity or business recovery plan).

6.1 Major Players in Disaster Recovery

- The organization itself.
- Application software vendors (who may need to provide replacement application software).
- IT and business area personnel (business area personnel are often forgotten, but somebody must do the work after the ability to process data is restored).
- Disaster recovery service provider (who is happy to provide disaster recovery services for a fee).
- Provisions/hardware vendors (replacement hardware or supplies may be needed).
- Senior management (who must support the disaster recovery plan or nothing will happen).

6.2 Steps in Disaster Recovery

- Assess risks.
- Identify mission-critical applications.
- Determine responsibilities of the personnel.
- Develop a plan.
- Test the plan.

Question 6-1   FR-00176

Conroe Company is a brokerage and commodities trading firm with customers all over the U.S. and in many foreign countries. Conroe has a formal disaster recovery plan that has been approved by its Board of Directors. The plan consists of a contracted cold site across the street from its main office building; processing will be transferred to that cold site if a disaster occurs. Which of the following statements with respect to Conroe's disaster recovery plan is/are correct?

I.   Conroe must have its disaster recovery plan certified by its external auditors.

II. Conroe's disaster recovery plan is more than sufficient given the nature of its business and the fact that the probability of a disaster occurring is considered to be minimal by the Board of Directors.

III. Conroe's disaster plan does not need to be tested since it will be relatively simple to transfer its data and programs to the cold site since it is so close.

    1. I only is correct.

    2. I and II only are correct.

    3. I and III only are correct.

    4. None of the statements are correct.

? Related Questions

For related questions, go to the online question bank:

➤ FR-00760

6.3   Split-Mirror Backup

Split-Mirror backups use a remote server to back up large amounts of data offline that can be restored in the event of a disaster.

6.4   Data Backup and Recovery Procedures

Some organizations contract with outside providers for disaster recovery services; the major factor under consideration is available hardware and telecommunication services.

6.4.1   Internal Disaster Recovery

Some organizations that require instantaneous resumption of processing after a disaster (e.g., banks, brokerage houses) provide their own duplicate facilities in separate locations.

6.4.2   Multiple Data Center Backups

Some organizations with multiple data centers plan to use one data center to back up another, assuming that there is enough capacity to process the essential applications. Several types of backups can be used to recover lost data, including:

■ **Full Backup**

A full backup is an exact copy of the entire database. Full backups are time-consuming, so most organizations only do full backups weekly and supplement them with daily partial backups.

■ **Partial Backup**

There are two types of partial backups possible:

- An *incremental* backup involves copying only the data items that have changed since the last backup. This produces a set of incremental backup files, each containing the results of one day's transactions.

- A *differential* backup copies all changes made since the last full backup. Thus, each new differential backup file contains the cumulative effects of all activity since the last full backup. Consequently, except for the first day following a full backup, daily differential backups take longer than incremental backups.

6.4.3. Alternative Processing Facilities

■ **Cold Site**

A cold site is a disaster recovery facility that does not have equipment and operating system software available. All that is provided is the infrastructure. The organization must provide everything else.

■ **Hot Site**

A hot site is a disaster recovery facility that does have equipment and operating system software available. The client must provide its application software and its data, and may provide its own operating system software in addition to the base operating system (all operating systems are not the same). Processing is normally restored faster with a hot site than with a cold site. Hot sites cost more than cold sites. There can also be situations in which entire data centers are replicated for instantaneous recovery or transfer of operations (this does not come cheaply).

■ **Warm Site**

A warm site is a facility that is already stocked with all the hardware necessary to create a reasonable facsimile of the primary data center. The advantage of the warm backup site is that restoration can be accomplished in a reasonable amount of time. The disadvantage is the cost of maintaining a contract with the facility to keep hardware up to date with what is at the organization's data center. The warm backup site is the compromise between the hot backup site and the cold backup site.

Question 6-2   FR-00758

Which of the below describes an off-site location that has all the electrical connections and other physical requirements for data processing, but it does not have the actual equipment?

1. Warm site
2. Hot site
3. Cold site
4. Freezing site

Task-Based Simulations

Task-Based Simulation: Written Communication

Prime FL, Inc, is a Florida-based company currently working on its disaster recovery plan. John Gordon, the company controller, has been given a large budget for this project, but he is unclear whether a *cold, hot,* or *warm site* is the right decision for his environment. As the *disaster recovery specialist*, draft a memo to John Gordon discussing the benefits of each site in order to assist him with his decision.

Type your communication in the response area below.

REMINDER: Your response will be graded for technical content and writing skills. Technical content will be evaluated for information that is helpful to the intended audience and clearly relevant to the issue. Writing skills will be evaluated for development, organization, and the appropriate expression of ideas in professional correspondence. Use an appropriate business format with a clear introduction, body, and conclusion. Do not convey information in the form of a table, bullet-point list, or other abbreviated presentation.

Memorandum

To: John Gordon, Controller
Re: Backup Solutions

Explanation

The purpose of this memo is to provide you with information regarding *disaster recovery* offsite location options and how they would be advantageous to Prime FL, Inc.

Disaster recovery and offsite locations consist of plans for continuing operations in the event of destruction of program and data files, as well as processing capability. Small outages should be reestablished at the original site; however, you should plan for an offsite location should Prime FL not be available due to a disaster.

Along with the cost involved, in order to make the right decision on which site is the correct for Prime FL, you will have to decide how urgently you will need to get your data, network, and users up and running.

A *hot site* is the most complete offsite option as well as the most costly. It would be fully equipped and would be ready to take over Prime FL's data processing in a matter of hours, as the backup copies of your essential data files would also be maintained at the same location. This would be the best option for a quicker recovery.

A *cold site* would have all the electrical connections and other physical requirements for data processing, but it would not have the actual equipment. Cold sites usually require one to three days to be made operational because equipment would have to be acquired. This would be the cheapest option for an offsite location.

A *warm site* is a combination between a *hot site* and a *cold site*. A *warm site* facility would already be stocked with all the hardware it takes to create a reasonable duplicate of what you have in your primary data center. The difference is that it would not maintain a copy of your data backup and it would have to be shipped to the offsite location. A restoration would be accomplished in a reasonable amount of time. Prime FL would still have a continued cost because a maintenance contract would have to be kept with the facility to keep hardware up-to-date.

In today's world, for a substantial organization not to have an offsite location as part of your disaster recovery plan is very risky. As budget does not seem to be an obstacle for Prime FL, Inc., I would suggest an implementation of a *hot site*.

I hope I have provided you with enough information to make an educated decision regarding which option would be best suited for Prime FL, Inc.

1 The Role of Input, Processing, and Output Controls

1.1 Input Controls

Input controls verify that transaction data is valid, complete, and accurate. Input controls may include data validation at the field level, prenumbered forms, and well-defined source data preparation procedures.

1.2 Processing Controls

Processing controls verify that all transactions are processing correctly during file maintenance. Key processing controls include data matching, use of file labels, recalculation of batch totals, cross-footing and zero-balance tests, write-protection mechanisms, and data processing integrity procedures.

1.3 Output Controls

Output controls verify the accuracy and integrity of reports. Output controls include review of output, reconciliation procedures, external data reconciliation, and output encryption.

1.4 Correctly Functioning Controls

Correctly functioning controls are designed to ensure completeness, accuracy, and continuous processing integrity.

Question 1-1   FR-00166

Macedonia Corporation's mainframe programming and operations staff is in an uproar. They have heard that the internal auditors are planning to insist upon all sorts of controls on the systems and programming activity, and they feel that these controls will cause them nothing but trouble. What sort of controls might Macedonia's internal auditors reasonably require?

I.   Input controls that require that certain key data be validated.

II. Input controls that require that all input data be processed in batches and that batch totals be maintained and verified for all batches.

III. Output controls that require that all reports be printed and manually distributed to end users through inter-office mail.

    1. I, II, and III are correct.

    2. I and II only are correct.

    3. I only is correct.

    4. II only is correct.

? Related Questions

For related questions, go to the online question bank:

➤ FR-00264

2   Design and Operating Effectiveness of Application Controls

2.1   Information Technology Controls

IT controls related to the use of information technology resources should be established, including:

- Appropriate segregation of duties
- Procedures that include design and use of adequate documents and records
- Limit access to assets
- Effective performance management
- Information processing controls
- Design and use of electronic and paper documents
- Implementation of security measures and contingency plans

2.2   Effectiveness of Control Policies

To minimize failures and reduce cost overruns, while substantially improving system efficiency and effectiveness, the following principles of control should be applied to systems development:

- Strategic master plan: Developed and updated yearly. It shows the projects that must be completed to achieve long-range company goals and addresses the company's hardware, software, personnel, and infrastructure requirements.
- Data processing schedule: To maximize the use of scarce computer resources, all data processing tasks should be organized according to a data processing schedule.
- Steering committee: Should be formed to guide and oversee systems development and acquisition.
- System performance measurements: For a system to be evaluated properly, it must be assessed using system performance measurements.

3   Roles and Responsibilities of Information Technology Professionals

The roles and responsibilities of IT professionals are defined by individual organizations, and job titles and responsibilities can vary widely.

3.1   Executive

Executive roles include chief information officers (CIOs) and chief technology officers (CTOs).

3.2 Management

Management includes senior IT executives, directors, and managers who usually report to the CIO or CTO. Titles in the real world can vary widely and do not necessarily indicate specific functions.

3.3 Programmers/Administrators/Analysts

- System analysts.
- Application programmers.
- System programmers. (In mainframe environments, system programmers maintain the operating system; in non-mainframe environments, operating system maintenance may be done by a system administrator. The functions can be essentially the same even if the titles are different.)
- Security administrators.
- Database administrators (are different from data administrators).

3.4 Segregation of Duties

Segregation of duties is defined as dividing responsibilities for different portions of a transaction (authorization, recording, and custody) among several different people or departments.

Within the IT department, the duties of system analysts and computer programmers, computer operators, and security administrators should be kept separate as much as possible.

Question 3-1   FR-00156

Lisa Company has an Information Technology department comprised of systems analysts, programmers, and operations personnel. It is considering implementing a database management system and obtaining the appropriate personnel to support that system. Which of the following statements is/are correct?

I. Lisa will not need a database administrator because the database management system will need no maintenance or support.

II. Lisa will need a data administrator to apply system upgrades to the database management system.

III. Lisa will not need any additional special expertise at all. Its existing programmers will be able to handle maintenance and support of the database management system.

1. I only is correct.
2. II only is correct.
3. I and III only are correct.
4. None of the statements are correct.

Related Questions

For related questions, go to the online question bank:

➤ FR-00135
➤ FR-00267

4 Design and Effectiveness of Information Technology

Controls can be manual (performed by a person without making direct use of automated systems) or automated (performed by an automated system, without interference of a person).

Controls can also be preventive (e.g., security awareness training, firewalls), detective (e.g., anti-virus, system monitoring), or corrective (e.g., backup data restore).

1 Fundamental Risks Related to Systems Development and Maintenance

Risks can be assessed and to some extent managed. Access, data, and procedural controls are all important tools of risk management.

1.1 Technology Risk

Four general types of risks associated with information technology systems:

1.1.1 Strategic Risk

Risk of choosing an inappropriate technology.

1.1.2 Operating Risk

Risk of doing the right things in the wrong way.

1.1.3 Financial Risk

Risk of having financial resources lost, wasted, or stolen.

1.1.4 Information Risk

Risk of loss of data integrity, incomplete transactions, or hackers.

Question 1-1   FR-00215

Each of the following represents a risk or challenge of e-commerce and Web commerce, *except*:

1. An inability to authenticate the identity of buyers and sellers.
2. Maintaining privacy and confidentiality of information.
3. Effecting a secure exchange of money for goods and services provided.
4. Incompatible encryption systems, resulting in faulty orders.

---

2 Managing IT Risk

2.1 IT Risk

In general, a risk is the possibility of harm or loss. IT risk is the business risk associated with the use, ownership, operation, involvement, influence, and adoption of IT within an enterprise.

2.2 Risk IT Framework

ISACA developed the Risk IT Framework to achieve three objectives:

1. Integrate management of IT risk into the overall risk management of the enterprise.
2. Make well-informed decisions about the nature and extent of the risk, the risk appetite, and risk tolerance.
3. Develop a response to the risk.

2.3 Categories of IT Risk

ISACA also sorts IT risk into three categories:

1. IT Benefit/Value Enablement Risk
2. IT Program and Project Delivery Risk
3. IT Operations and Service Delivery Risk

3 Risk Assessment

Before risks can be managed, they must be assessed. The steps in risk assessment are to:

1. identify threats;
2. evaluate the probability that the threat will occur;
3. evaluate the exposure in terms of potential loss from each threat;
4. identify the controls that could guard against the threats;
5. evaluate the costs and benefits of implementing controls; and
6. implement controls that are determined to be cost effective.

4 Risks Related to New Technology

AICPA published lessons learned that stressed the following points when implementing new technology:

- Define the integration points to the governance processes.
- Define and manage planning data.
- Define and publicize the planning calendar.
- Realize that timing is essential.
- Clearly define roles and responsibilities.
- Communicate data and messages well.

5 Risks Related to Legacy Systems

5.1 Reasons for Persistence of Legacy Systems

- Investment in deployment
- Investment in training
- Dependencies on supportive technology
- Dependencies built on the legacy product
- Risk over reward

5.2 Risks of Legacy Systems

- Lack of vendor support
- Old "threatscape"
- Code reutilization
- Educated hackers
- Patch lag
- Evolving hacker tools
- Dependency on insecure platform

5.3 Mitigating Risk in Legacy Systems

Mitigating risks related to legacy systems can be accomplished either through isolating the system and/or virtual patches.

6 Information System Testing Strategies

Software testing is intended to find defects created during development, determine the level of quality, and ensure that the end product meets business and user requirements. An effective testing strategy includes automated, manual, and exploratory tests to efficiently reduce risk, including unit tests and integration tests (both bottom-up and top-down integration testing approaches).

6.1 Guidelines for Successful Testing

- Specify testing objectives explicitly.
- Identify categories of users for the software and develop a profile for each.
- Build robust software that is designed to test itself.
- Use effective formal reviews as a filter prior to testing.
- Conduct formal technical reviews to assess the test strategy and test cases.
- Develop a continuous improvement approach for the testing process.

Question 6-1 FR-00212

Company B has been on its current information technology system for 15 years. The CIO thinks that it is time for a change and puts together a project team to start brainstorming ideas for either upgrades to the system or implementation of a new system. Which of the following would be a reason in support of the change?

1. Legacy system possesses less sophisticated security mechanisms.
2. Vendor agrees to continue ongoing support for the legacy system.
3. Special product customizations for every product are designed into the legacy system.
4. The legacy system can run in any environment.

? Related Questions

For related questions, go to the online question bank:

➤ FR-00293
➤ FR-00297
➤ FR-00298

V | Operations Management

1 Financial and Nonfinancial Performance Measures

1.1 Financial Measures

The following are used as a financial measure of performance:

- Profit is the amount of income generated after expenses.

- Return on investment is the income generated based on a given investment (e.g., total assets employed, stockholders' equity).

- Variance analysis compares actual performance to expected performance.

- Balance scorecard is a framework used to convert an entity's strategic objectives into a set of performance measures.

1.2 Nonfinancial Measures

1.2.1 External Benchmarks

External benchmarks/productivity measures include:

- Total factor productivity ratios (TFPs) reflect the quantity of all output produced relative to the costs of all inputs used.

- Partial productivity ratios (PPRs) reflect the quantity of output produced relative to the quantity of individual inputs used.

1.2.2 Internal Benchmarks

Internal benchmarks/techniques for analyzing problems:

- A control chart is a graphical tool used to plot a comparison of actual results by batch to an acceptable range to determine improvement or deterioration of quality conformance.

- A Pareto diagram is used to plot the frequency of defects from the highest to lowest frequency.

- Cause-and-effect (fishbone) diagrams are used to identify recurring and costly defects and then break down the problems that led to the individual defects.

1.3 Characteristics of Effective Performance Measures

Effective performance measures promote the achievement of goals. Typically, the characteristics of those measures:

- relate to the goals of the organization;

- balance long- and short-term issues;

- reflect management of key activities, sometimes referred to as critical success factors in the balanced scorecard;

- are under the control or influence of the employee;

- are understood by the employee;

- are used to both evaluate and reward the employee or otherwise constructively influence behavior;

- are objective and easily measured; and

- are used consistently.

Question 1-1   FR-00794

The Long Haul Trucking Company is developing metrics for its drivers. The company computes variable costs of each load based upon miles driven and allocates fixed costs based upon time consumed. Load costing standards consider safe driving speeds and Department of Transportation regulations on hours of service (the amount of time the driver can be on duty or drive). The most effective metric for driver performance would likely be:

1. Contribution per mile driven.

2. Gross margin per mile driven.

3. Achievement of delivered loads in allowed times.

4. Percentage increase in delivered loads below standard.

---

2 ROI and ROA

2.1 ROI

- Return on investment (ROI) provides for the assessment of a company's percentage return relative to its capital investment risk.

- ROI is calculated as follows:

> ROI = Income / Investment capital
>
> OR
>
> ROI = Profit margin × Investment turnover

2.2 ROA

- Return on assets (ROA) is similar to ROI, except that ROA uses average total assets in the denominator rather than invested capital.

- ROA is calculated as follows:

$$\text{Return on total assets ratio} = \frac{\text{Net income}}{\text{Average total assets}}$$

Question 2-1   FR-00254

The following information pertains to Quest Co.'s Gold Division for Year 4:

Sales	$311,000
Variable cost	250,000
Traceable fixed costs	50,000
Average invested capital	40,000
Imputed interest rate	10%

Quest's return on investment was:

1. 10%
2. 13.33%
3. 27.5%
4. 30%

3 ROE and DuPont Ratios

3.1 ROE

A measure of profitability, return on equity (ROE) is the amount of net income returned as a percentage of shareholder's equity.

$$ROE = \frac{\text{Net income}}{\text{Equity}}$$

3.2 DuPont Ratio

The DuPont ratio is a means for breaking down ROE into three components:

DuPont ROE = Net profit margin × Asset turnover × Financial leverage

$$= \frac{\text{Net income}}{\text{Sales}} \times \frac{\text{Sales}}{\text{Average total assets}} \times \frac{\text{Average total assets}}{\text{Equity}}$$

3.3 Extended DuPont Ratio

The extended DuPont ratio breaks down ROE into five components:

Extended DuPont ROE = Tax burden × Interest burden × Operating income margin × Asset turnover × Financial leverage

$$= \frac{\text{Net income}}{\text{Pretax income}} \times \frac{\text{Pretax income}}{\text{EBIT}} \times \frac{\text{EBIT}}{\text{Sales}} \times \frac{\text{Sales}}{\text{Average total assets}} \times \frac{\text{Average total assets}}{\text{Equity}}$$

4 Residual Income and Economic Value Added

4.1 Residual Income

■ The formula for residual income is as follows:

Residual income = Net income (from the income statement) − Required return

Where:

Required return = Net book value (Equity) × Hurdle rate

- The hurdle rate used is the cost of equity, which can be established by management or calculated using any of the traditional methods (CAPM, DCF, BYRP).

4.2   Economic Value Added

- The formula for Economic Value Added™ (EVA™) is as follows:

> Economic value added = Net operating profit after taxes − Required return

Where:

> Required return = Investment × Cost of capital

- The cost of capital used is typically the weighted average cost of capital (WACC).

Question 4-1   FR-00262

Following is information relating to Kew Co.'s Vale Division for Year 4:

Sales	$500,000
Variable cost	300,000
Traceable fixed costs	50,000
Average invested capital	100,000
Imputed interest rate	6%

Vale's residual income was:

1. $144,000
2. $150,000
3. $156,000
4. $200,000

? Related Questions

For related questions, go to the online question bank:

➤ FR-00152
➤ FR-00258

---

1 Cost Objects

Cost objects (objectives) are resources or activities that serve as the basis for management decisions.

1.1 Product Costs

- Product costs comprise all costs related to the manufacturing of a product.
- Components of product costs include direct material, direct labor, and manufacturing overhead applied.
- Product costs are inventoriable and traceable (e.g., work in process inventory, finished goods inventory, and cost of goods sold).

1.2 Period Costs

Period costs (e.g., selling, general and administrative expenses) are expensed in the period in which they are incurred and are not inventoriable.

1.3 Manufacturing Costs

- Manufacturing costs (e.g., direct materials, direct labor, and manufacturing overhead) include all costs associated with the manufacturing of a product.
- Manufacturing costs include both direct and indirect costs.

1.4 Nonmanufacturing Costs

- Nonmanufacturing costs are costs that do not relate to the manufacturing of a product, such as advertising costs and salaries of sales personnel.
- Nonmanufacturing costs are expensed in the period incurred.

2 Tracing Costs to Cost Objects

2.1 Direct Costs

- A direct cost can be easily traced to the cost pool or cost object.
- Direct costs include direct raw materials and direct labor.

2.2 Indirect Costs

■ An indirect cost is not easily traced to the cost pool or cost object.

■ Also known as manufacturing overhead, indirect costs include indirect materials, indirect labor, and other indirect costs (e.g., machine maintenance costs).

■ Indirect costs are allocated to cost pools/objects using cost drivers that have a significant relationship to the incurrence of these costs.

3 Cost Behavior

3.1 Variable Costs

■ A variable cost varies in total as production volume increases or decreases, but remains constant on a per unit basis.

■ Direct materials and direct labor are variable costs.

3.2 Fixed Costs

■ A fixed cost remains constant in total, regardless if the production volume increases or decreases, but varies per unit.

■ Depreciation would be classified as a fixed cost.

■ Over a long-run time horizon, any cost can be considered variable.

3.3 Semi-variable Costs (Mixed Costs)

Semi-variable costs are costs that contain both fixed and variable components (e.g., water utilities, where there is a fixed monthly charge plus a variable rate per gallon used).

3.4 Relevant Range

■ The relevant range is the (graphical) range for which the assumptions of a cost driver are valid.

■ Any cost driver activity that is outside the relevant range cannot be used to allocate costs to objects.

Question 3-1   FR-00193

Applewhite Corporation, a manufacturing company, is analyzing its cost structure in a project to achieve some cost savings. Which of the following statements is/are correct?

I.   The cost of the raw materials in Applewhite's products is considered a variable cost.

II. The cost of the depreciation of Applewhite's factory machinery is considered a variable cost because Applewhite uses an accelerated depreciation method for both book and income tax purposes.

III. The cost of electricity for Applewhite's manufacturing facility is considered a fixed cost, even if the cost of the electricity has both variable and fixed components.

    1. I, II, and III are correct.

    2. I only is correct.

    3. II and III only are correct.

    4. None of the listed choices is correct.

? Related Questions

For related questions, go to the online question bank:

➤ FR-00183

➤ FR-00270

➤ FR-00272

➤ FR-00295

4 Cost Accumulation Systems

Cost accumulation systems are used to assign costs to products. Use job order costing when the cost object is a custom order (a batch of business cards). Use process costing when the cost object is a mass-produced homogeneous product (canned vegetables).

5 Cost of Goods Manufactured and Sold

5.1 Cost of Goods Manufactured

The cost of goods manufactured statement accounts for the manufacturing costs of the products completed during the period. Cost of goods manufactured is used as part of the cost of goods sold computation.

Beginning WIP		XXX
Direct materials used	XXX	
Direct labor	XXX	
Factory overhead *applied**	XXX	
Total manufacturing costs		XXX
Manufacturing costs available		XXX
Less: Ending WIP		<XXX>
Cost of goods manufactured		XXX

* Factory overhead is applied based on a predetermined rate. In traditional costing, estimated costs are divided by a common divisor, such as direct labor hours, direct labor costs, or machine hours. The formula for the traditional overhead application method is as follows:

$$\text{Predetermined OH rate} = \frac{\text{Estimated total overhead costs}}{\text{Estimated total direct labor hours or other divisors}}$$

5.2 Cost of Goods Sold

Cost of goods sold is the amount matched against sales revenue as part of income determination.

Beginning finished goods inventory	XXX
Cost of goods manufactured	XXX
= Cost of goods available for sale	XXX
Less: Ending finished goods inventory	<XXX>
Cost of goods sold	XXX

If overhead applied is greater than the total actual overhead costs incurred, we say overhead is overapplied. If the applied overhead is less than the actual, we have underapplied overhead. Overapplied overhead is closed to cost of goods sold as a credit to the expense. Underapplied overhead is closed to cost of goods sold as a debit to the expense.

Question 5-1 FR-00203

Culpepper Corporation had the following inventories at the beginning and end of the month of January:

	January 1	January 31
Finished goods	$125,000	$117,000
Work-in-process	235,000	251,000
Direct materials	134,000	124,000

The following additional manufacturing data was available for the month of January:

Direct materials purchased	$189,000
Purchase returns and allowances	1,000
Transportation in	3,000
Direct labor	400,000
Actual factory overhead	175,000

Culpepper Corporation applies factory overhead at a rate of 40 percent of direct labor cost, and any overapplied or underapplied factory overhead is deferred until the end of the year. Culpepper's balance in its factory overhead control account at the end of January was:

1. $15,000 overapplied.
2. $15,000 underapplied.
3. $5,000 underapplied.
4. $5,000 overapplied.

Related Questions

For related questions, go to the online question bank:

- FR-00232
- FR-00284
- FR-00296

6 Job Order Costing

Job order costing is a cost accumulation or product costing method that involves unique or easily identifiable units. This method is used when manufacturing custom products such as customized cars, boats and houses.

- Costs are allocated to a specific job as it moves through the manufacturing process.
- Job cost records or job orders accumulate all costs for a specific job with data obtained from material requisitions and labor time cards.
- Once the job is complete, the total cost is readily available on the job cost record.

7 Process Costing

Process costing accumulates costs by department or process. Two methods are used: FIFO and weighted average. Generally, equivalent units and cost per equivalent unit must be calculated. Unit and cost flow assumptions are specific to each method.

7.1 Application

Process costing is used in those instances in which homogenous units of output are produced and average costing is appropriate. Applications include fuel refining, chemical processing, and paper production.

Transfers in from other departments are always considered 100 percent complete. The transfer in costs of direct material from a previous department are treated as direct materials (DM), even though they are called "transfer in" costs or "previous department" costs.

Direct material added at the beginning of or during a second or later process may either be 100 percent complete or "partially complete," depending on how much work has been done on that component of the process.

Any material added at the (very) end of a process will not be in work in process inventory at the month end.

7.2 Equivalent Units

An equivalent unit of direct material, direct labor, or conversion costs is equal to the amount of direct material, direct labor, or conversion costs necessary to complete one unit of production. Equivalent units of production may be computed using either first-in first-out (FIFO) or weighted average assumptions. The FIFO approach specifically accounts for work to be completed during a period, while the weighted average approach accounts for work completed during the period as well as the work performed last period on this period's beginning inventory.

7.2.1 FIFO (Three Steps)

Beginning WIP × % to be completed	XXX
Units completed—Beginning WIP	XXX
Ending WIP × % completed	XXX
Equivalent units	XXX

7.2.2 Weighted Average (Two Steps)

Units completed	XXX
Ending WIP × % completed	XXX
Equivalent units	XXX

7.3 Cost per Equivalent Units

Cost per equivalent unit is computed by dividing total costs by equivalent units. FIFO anticipates using only current period costs, while the weighted average approach uses both costs of beginning inventory and current period costs as follows:

7.3.1 FIFO

$$FIFO = \frac{Current\ cost\ only}{Equivalent\ units}$$

7.3.2 Weighted Average

$$Weighted\ average = \frac{Beginning\ cost\ +\ Current\ cost}{Equivalent\ units}$$

7.4 Spoilage

Equivalent units added for a month are usually less than the actual units added during the month as a result of problems with the production process. This is the result of spoilage or shrinkage, which is usually factored in automatically. There are two types of spoilage:

- **Normal spoilage:** This occurs under regular operating conditions and is charged to factory overhead (inventory cost).

- **Abnormal spoilage:** This does not occur under normal operating conditions and is treated as a period expense. Examples of abnormal spoilage include floods, fire damage, and spoilage materially in excess of standard caused by inefficient equipment or labor.

Question 7-1   FR-00292

On May 1, Mass Manufacturing had 100 units in its beginning work-in-process that were 60 percent complete. The company completed 500 units during May and had 200 units in its ending inventory on May 31 that were 40 percent complete. Using FIFO or weighted average, the equivalent units of production would be:

	Weighted Average	FIFO
1.	520	580
2.	580	520
3.	560	620
4.	620	560

Question 7-2   FR-00223

Penn Manufacturing Corporation uses a process costing system to manufacture printers for PCs. The following information summarizes operations for its NoToner model during the quarter ending September 30, Year 1:

	Units	Direct Labor
Work-in-process inventory, July 1	100	$ 50,000
Started during the quarter	500	
Completed during the quarter	400	
Work-in-process inventory, September 30	200	
Costs added during the quarter		$ 775,000

Beginning work-in-process inventory was 50 percent complete for direct labor. Ending work-in-process inventory was 75 percent complete for direct labor. What is the total value of the direct labor in the ending work-in-process inventory using the weighted average method?

1. $183,000
2. $194,000
3. $225,000
4. $210,000

? Related Questions

For related questions, go to the online question bank:

➤ FR-00213
➤ FR-00244
➤ FR-00249
➤ FR-00253
➤ FR-00282
➤ FR-00288
➤ FR-00290

8 Activity-Based Costing (ABC)

8.1 Defined

Activity-based costing (ABC) is a costing system that divides production into activities where costs are accumulated (cost pools) and allocated to the product based on the level of activity demanded by the product.

8.2 Characteristics

ABC tends to increase both the number of cost pools (e.g., production orders, material handling, etc.) and allocation bases (e.g., number of production orders, pounds, etc.), whereas a traditional cost system would use one cost base and one allocation base (e.g., factory overhead/direct labor hours).

8.3 Service Cost Allocation

When using ABC, companies may allocate service department costs to production or user departments and ultimately the final products produced. Service costs may be allocated using the direct method or step-down method.

8.3.1 Direct Method

Under the direct method, each service department's total costs are allocated to the production departments directly without recognizing that service departments themselves may also use the services from other service departments.

8.3.2 Step-Down Method

Under the step-down method, service department costs are allocated to production departments as well as other service departments that use a given service department's services. The allocation to other service departments is done through a step-down allocation process.

Question 8-1   FR-00274

Nobis Company uses an ABC system. Which of the following statements is/are correct with respect to ABC?

I. Departmental costing systems are a refinement of ABC systems.

II. ABC systems are useful in manufacturing, but not in merchandising or service industries.

III. ABC systems can eliminate cost distortions because ABC develops cost drivers that have a cause-and-effect relationship with the activities performed.

    1. I, II, and III are correct.

    2. II and III only are correct.

    3. III only is correct.

    4. None of the listed choices are correct.

---

9 Joint Product Costing and By-product Costing

In joint product costing (JPC), two or more products are produced from the same common raw material. Joint product costing methods are used to segregate costs associated with each product jointly produced by the same process. Examples include the fuel refining process that produces various octane levels, and lumber processing that produces construction and nonconstruction-grade products.

9.1 Relative Sales Value at Split-off Approach

Joint costs are allocated to joint products based on the relative sales value at split-off.

9.1.1 Example

Joint costs $1,000	
Product A: Sales value at split-off	$10,000
Product B: Sales value at split-off	$30,000
Total	$40,000

9.1.2 Computation

Hence, 1/4 of the $1,000 joint costs, or $250, is assigned to Product A, and 3/4 of the $1,000 joint costs, or $750, is assigned to Product B.

9.2 Net Realizable Value Approach

Costs added after the split-off point (separable costs) must be subtracted from the final selling price to arrive at the net realizable value (NRV).

9.2.1 Example

	NRV
Joint costs $6,000	
Product A: Final selling price $12,000, after split-off cost $2,000 =	$10,000
Product B: Final selling price $25,000, after split-off cost $5,000 =	$20,000
Total	$30,000

9.2.2 Computation

Hence, the NRV of Product A is $10,000 and Product B is $20,000. Therefore, 1/3 of the $6,000 joint costs, or $2,000, would be assigned to Product A, and 2/3 of the $6,000 joint costs, or $4,000, would be assigned to Product B.

9.3 Service Departments Cost Allocation to Joint Products

Service department costs are allocated to joint products based on the joint products proportional unit-volume relationship.

9.3.1 Example

The janitorial service department provides services for Products A and B. The department incurs costs of $6,000, which are allocated to each product based on the joint products unit-volume relationship.

Product A	10,000 gal.
Product B	20,000 gal.
Total	30,000 gal.

Janitorial service department costs are allocated as follows:

Product A: (10,000 / 30,000) × $6,000	$2,000
Product B: (20,000 / 30,000) × $6,000	$4,000
Total	$6,000

9.4 By-products

By-products represent outputs of minor value incidental to a manufacturing process. Accounting can take one of two forms:

1. Revenue applied to the main product as a cost reduction

2. Miscellaneous income

B   Cost Accounting

Question 9-1 FR-00123

Dallas Company produces joint products, TomL and JimmyJ, each of which incurs separable production costs after the split-off point. Information concerning a batch produced at a $200,000 joint cost before split-off follows:

Product	Separable Costs	Sales Value
TomL	$ 10,000	$ 80,000
JimmyJ	20,000	50,000
	$ 30,000	$ 130,000

What is the joint cost assigned to TomL if costs are assigned using relative net realizable value?

1. $60,000
2. $140,000
3. $48,000
4. $200,000

Question 9-2 FR-00286

Houston Corporation has two products, Astros and Texans, with the following volume information:

	Volume
Product Astros	20,000 gal
Product Texans	10,000 gal
Total	30,000 gal

The joint cost to produce the two products is $120,000. What portion of the joint cost will each product be allocated if the allocation is performed by volume?

1. $100,000 and $0
2. $80,000 and $40,000
3. $40,000 and $80,000
4. $50,000 and $50,000

Related Questions

For related questions, go to the online question bank:

➤ FR-00294

© Becker Professional Education Corporation. All rights reserved.

1 Business Process Management

■ Business process management is also known as BPM and promotes continuous improvement in business processes.

■ There are many generic BPM methodologies, but the most recognized method is **P**lan, **D**o, **C**heck, **A**ct (**PDCA**).

■ Measures can be financial or nonfinancial and should correlate directly to the managed process to determine progress toward expectations.

■ Benefits of process management include improved efficiency, effectiveness, and agility for the organization.

2 Shared Services, Outsourcing, and Offshore Operations

■ Shared services is a consolidation of redundant services in an organization or group of affiliates. While consolidation of redundant services leads to efficiency, it may result in service flow disruption or failure demand. Shared services is an "in-house" solution.

■ Outsourcing services involves contracting with a third party to provide a service. Risks pertaining to outsourcing services include inferior quality of service and the security of information, which may be compromised.

■ Offshore operations is the outsourcing of services to providers outside of the country. All outsourcing risks plus lack of control caused by proximity issues and language barriers are potential risks.

3 Selecting and Implementing Improvement Initiatives

■ Rational and irrational methods may be used to select improvement initiatives.

■ Rational assessments are structured and systematic, while irrational methods are intuitive and emotional.

Question 3-1 FR-00818

Failure demand is:

1. The concept that some modest amount of failure is allowed in a manufacturing process because the cost of zero-error-rate is too high.
2. Demand for a company's product due to the inferior quality and subsequent failure of a competitor's product.
3. Demand for services in a shared-service environment due to failure to provide quality service to the customer the first time.
4. Demand for parts and supplies inventory to support the provision of warranty repairs.

---

4 Business Process Reengineering

- Business process reengineering (BPR) seeks radical change by entirely changing the design and operation of business processes.

- BPR is different from business process management (BPM). BPM seeks incremental rather than radical changes.

- The basic idea behind BPR is to create a fresh start by effectively "wiping the slate clean" and reassessing the process from the ground up.

5 Management Philosophies and Techniques for Performance Improvement

5.1 Just-in-Time (JIT)

The concept of Just-in-Time (JIT) inventory systems is that resources will be introduced to the manufacturing process only as they are needed. An item is produced only when it is requested further downstream in the production cycle. JIT systems serve to make organizations more efficient and better managed. JIT assumes that maintaining inventory does not add value.

5.2 Quality (Control)

Quality is broadly defined by the marketplace as a product's ability to meet or exceed customer expectations. The cost of quality is classified into two components: conformance costs and nonconformance costs.

5.2.1 Conformance Costs

Conformance costs are incurred to ensure quality standards are being met and are classified as either prevention costs or appraisal costs.

- Appraisal costs are costs incurred to discover and remove defective parts before shipment. Examples include statistical quality checks, testing, and inspection.

- Prevention costs are costs incurred to prevent the production of defective units. Examples include employee training, inspection, redesigning products and processes, and searching for higher-quality suppliers.

5.2.2 Nonconformance Costs

Nonconformance costs are the costs associated with not conforming to quality standards and are classified as internal failure costs or external failure costs.

- Internal failure costs are necessary to cure a defect discovered before the product is sent to the customer. Examples include rework labor costs, scrap, tooling changes, disposal costs, cost of a lost unit, and downtime.

- External failure costs are necessary to cure a defect discovered after the product is sent to the customer. Examples include warranty costs, costs for returning the good, liability claims, lost customers, and reengineering.

5.2.3 Total Quality Management

Total quality management (TQM) is an organizational commitment to customer-focused performance that stresses both quality and continuous improvement.

5.3 Lean Manufacturing

Lean manufacturing uses only those resources that are necessary to meet customer requirements or that add value to the production process.

- The focus is also on waste reduction and efficiency.

- Kaizen refers to continuous improvement efforts that improve the efficiency and effectiveness of organizations through greater operational control. Kaizen occurs at the manufacturing stage where the ongoing search for cost reductions takes the form of analysis of production processes to ensure that resource uses stay within target costs.

- An organization may implement process improvements by using activity-based costing (ABC) and activity-based management (ABM).

5.4 Demand Flow

Demand flow seeks to reduce waste by bringing resources into production as they are demanded rather than as they are scheduled for production. Demand flow blends the efficiencies of JIT with the effectiveness (customer-focused, value-added) goals of lean manufacturing.

5.5 Theory of Constraints

Theory of constraints (TOC) is a management philosophy that says organizations are impeded from achieving objectives by the existence of one or more constraints. The organization or project must be consistently operated in a manner that either works around or leverages the constraint. There are five steps to applying TOC:

1. **Identification of the Constraint:** Use of process charts or interviews results in identification of the constraint that produces suboptimal performance.

2. **Exploitation of the Constraint:** Planning around the constraint uses capacity that is potentially wasted by making or selling the wrong products, improper procedures in scheduling, etc.

3. **Subordinate Everything Else to the Above Decisions:** Management directs its efforts to improving the performance of the constraint.

4. **Elevate the Constraint:** Add capacity to overcome the constraint.

5. **Return to the First Step:** Reexamine the process to optimize the results. Remain cognizant that inertia can be a constraint.

5.6 Six Sigma

Six Sigma recommends the use of rigorous metrics in the evaluation of goal achievement and logically anticipates methodologies to improve current processes and develop new processes.

- Existing product and business process improvements (**DMAIC**)

  - **D**efine the problem
  - **M**easure key aspects of the current process
  - **A**nalyze data
  - **I**mprove or optimize current processes
  - **C**ontrol

- New product or business process development (**DMADV**)

  - **D**efine design goals
  - **M**easure CTQ (critical to quality issues)
  - **A**nalyze design alternatives
  - **D**esign optimization
  - **V**erify the design

Question 5-1   FR-00817

Jordan Inc. has adopted a new manufacturing management philosophy that requires that an item is produced only when it is requested downstream in the production cycle. Jordan has adopted which of the following?

1. Business process outsourcing
2. Shared services
3. Just-in-time inventory systems
4. DMAIC

Related Questions

For related questions, go to the online question bank:

➤ FR-00233
➤ FR-00281
➤ FR-00798
➤ FR-00819
➤ FR-00824

1 Budgets

1.1 Master Budgets

A master budget is a budget at one level of activity.

1.1.1 Design

A master budget (often referred to as a "static" budget) generally includes operating budgets and financial budgets.

1.1.2 Characteristics

The annual plan anticipates the coming year's activities that will contribute to the accomplishment of the long-term and short-term goals outlined in the company's strategic plan.

1.2 Flexible Budgets

Flexible budgets are budgets at several levels of activity.

1.2.1 Design

Flexible budgets are normally designed for a period of one year or less to accommodate the potential changing relationship between per unit revenues and costs.

1.2.2 Characteristics

Flexible budgets include consideration of revenue per unit, variable costs per unit, and fixed costs over the relevant range.

Question 1-1   FR-00265

Fulton Corporation manufactures and sells boxes of fish sticks. The static (master) budget and the actual results for May Year 1 were as follows:

	Actual	Static Budget
Unit sales	24,000	20,000
Sales	$264,000	$200,000
Variable costs of sales	158,400	120,000
Contribution margin	105,600	80,000
Fixed costs	(60,000)	(60,000)
Operating income	$ 45,600	$ 20,000

The operating income for Fulton Corporation using a flexible budget for May Year 1 was:

1. $36,000
2. $42,000
3. $38,000
4. $32,000

2 Operating vs. Financial Budgets

2.1   Operating Budgets

Operating budgets consist of the following budgets:

■ Sales budgets

■ Production budgets

- Direct materials budget
- Direct labor budget
- Factory overhead budget
- Cost of goods sold budget

■ Selling and administrative budgets

2.2   Financial Budgets

Financial budgets consist of the following budgets:

■ Pro forma financial statements

■ Cash budgets

Question 2-1
FR-00273

Budgets can be developed under any number of assumptions or methods. Which of the following statements regarding budgeting methods is true?

1. Variance analysis is not possible with a master budget.
2. Master budgets can only be constructed using an annual plan.
3. Flexible budgets are synonymous with variance analysis from standards.
4. Budgeting generally starts with sales forecasts.

Question 2-2
FR-00224

The Bronx Corporation is a manufacturing company with a budgeting system that includes a master budget and flexible budgets for various levels of production. Which of the following statements is/are correct?

I. Master budgets are normally confined to a single year for a single level of activity.

II. Flexible budgets are financial plans prepared in a manner that allows for adjustments for changes in production or sales and accurately reflects expected costs for the adjusted output.

III. Normally, the first step in the preparation of Bronx's master budget for a year would be the preparation of its production budget.

IV. The success of Bronx's budgeting program will depend on the degree to which its top management accepts the program and how its management uses the budgeted data.

1. I, II, and III are correct.
2. I, II, and IV are correct.
3. I and II only are correct.
4. All of the listed choices are correct.

? Related Questions

For related questions, go to the online question bank:

➤ FR-00250

3 Cash Budgets

A typical cash budget will be presented in the format:

> Beginning cash balance
>
> + Cash collections
> _____
>
> Total cash available
>
> - Cash payments
> _____
>
> Ending cash balance (before financing)
>
> + Financing (borrowings less interest payments less repayments)
> _____
>
> Ending cash balance (after financing)

Question 3-1   FR-00245

Rolling Wheels purchases bicycle components in the month prior to assembling them into bicycles. Assembly is scheduled one month prior to budgeted sales. Rolling pays 75% of component costs in the month of purchase and 25% of the costs in the following month. Component costs included in budgeted cost of sales are:

April	May	June	July	August
$ 5,000	$ 6,000	$ 7,000	$ 8,000	$ 8,000

What is Rolling's budgeted cash payments for components in May?

1. $5,750
2. $6,750
3. $7,750
4. $8,000

4 Variance Analysis

4.1   Variance Analysis

Variance analysis involves differences between budgeted (targeted or standard) and actual performance.

- Actual cost lower than standard produces a favorable variance.
- Actual cost higher than standard produces an unfavorable variance.

4.2   Expense Variances

Expense variances are calculated for:

- Direct material
- Direct labor
- Manufacturing overhead

4.3   Direct Materials and Direct Labor Variance

For direct materials and direct labor, two variances are calculated:

- Price and quantity variance
- Rate and efficiency variance

EQUATION FORMAT

DM price variance = Actual quantity purchased × (Actual price − Standard price)

DM quantity usage variance = Standard price × (Actual quantity used − Standard quantity allowed)

DL rate variance = Actual hours worked × (Actual rate − Standard rate)

DL efficiency variance = Standard rate × (Actual hours worked − Standard hours allowed)

TABULAR FORMAT

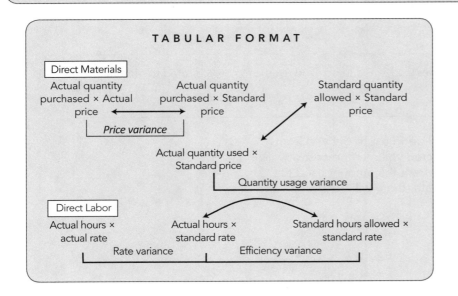

4.4 Manufacturing Overhead Variance

Overhead variances represent the analysis of any balance in the overhead account after overhead has been applied. Overapplied overhead (more credit) is favorable, while underapplied overhead (more debit) is unfavorable. The equations for the four overhead variances are as follows:

4.4.1 Variable Overhead Rate (Spending) Variance

VOH rate (spending) variance = Actual hours x (Actual rate − Standard rate)

Assuming a cost driver of labor hours, given the actual number of labor hours that were needed to produce a deliverable, this variance tells managers whether more or less was spent on variable overhead than what was expected.

4.4.2 Variable Overhead Efficiency (Usage) Variance

VOH efficiency (usage) variance = Standard rate x (Actual hours − Standard hours allowed for actual production volume)

The efficiency variance isolates the amount of total variable overhead variance that is due to using more or fewer labor hours than what was budgeted.

4.4.3 Fixed Overhead Budget (Spending) Variance

FOH budget (spending) variance = Actual fixed overhead − Budgeted fixed overhead

Companies budget an amount for fixed overhead costs every period, and this variance focuses at a high level on whether more or less was spent than budgeted.

4.4.4 Fixed Overhead Volume Variance

FOH volume variance = Budgeted fixed overhead − Standard fixed overhead cost allocated to production*

* based on Actual production x Standard rate

Fixed overhead costs are typically applied using a rate derived from budgeted fixed overhead costs and expected volume (the cost driver). When the actual volume produced differs from the amount used to calculate the fixed overhead application rate, there will be a variance.

4.5 Sales Variances

For sales variances:

- Actual sales prices higher (lower) than budgeted sales prices produce a favorable (unfavorable) variance.

- Actual units sold higher (lower) than budgeted units sold produce a favorable (unfavorable) variance.

4.5.1 Sales Price Variance (or Sales Revenue Flexible Budget Variance)

The sales price variance measures the aggregate impact of a selling price different from budget.

> Sales price variance = (Actual SP per unit − Budgeted SP per unit) × Actual sold units

4.5.2 Sales Volume Variance

The sales volume variance is a flexible budget variance that distills volume activity from other sales performance components. The basic sales volume variance is as follows:

$$\text{Sales volume variance} = \left(\begin{array}{c} \text{Actual} \\ \text{units sold} \end{array} - \begin{array}{c} \text{Budgeted} \\ \text{unit sales} \end{array} \right) \times \text{Standard contribution margin per unit}$$

Question 4-1   FR-00134

Flatbush Corporation has a standard costing system for each of its products. The standard direct material cost to produce a unit of its premier product Brook is 4 pounds of material at $2.50 per pound, or $10.00 per unit. During May Year 1, 8,400 pounds of material costing $20,160 were purchased and used to produce 2,000 units of Brook.

What was the materials usage variance for May Year 1?

1. $1,000 unfavorable.
2. $1,000 favorable.
3. $1,600 unfavorable.
4. $960 unfavorable.

Question 4-2   FR-00144

Bedford Corporation produces 2,500 units of its broadband router each month. Each unit is expected to require 4 labor hours at a cost of $10 per hour. Total labor cost was $104,500 for 9,500 hours worked.

What is the labor rate variance for the production of the router?

   1. $10,000 favorable.

   2. $10,000 unfavorable.

   3. $9,500 favorable.

   4. $9,500 unfavorable.

Question 4-3   FR-00164

Norwood Corporation produces a single product. The standard costs for one unit of its Bedford product are as follows:

Direct materials (6 pounds at $0.50 per pound)	$ 3
Direct labor (2 hours at $10 per hour)	20
Variable manufacturing overhead (2 hours at $5 per hour)	10
Total	$ 33

During October Year 2, 4,000 units of Bedford were produced. The costs associated with October operations were as follows:

Material purchased (36,000 pounds at $0.60 per pound)	$ 21,600
Material used in production (28,000 pounds)	
Direct labor (8,200 hours at $9.75 per hour)	79,950
Variable manufacturing overhead incurred	41,820

What is the variable overhead spending variance for Bedford for October Year 2?

   1. $4,200 favorable.

   2. $820 unfavorable.

   3. $1,820 unfavorable.

   4. $1,000 unfavorable.

? Related Questions

For related questions, go to the online question bank:

➤ FR-00124

➤ FR-00154

➤ FR-00194

➤ FR-00204

➤ FR-00268

➤ FR-00271

➤ FR-00275

➤ FR-00283

➤ FR-00285

5 Responsibility Segments

Responsibility segments, sometimes referred to as strategic business units (SBUs), are highly effective in establishing accountability for financial dimensions of the business. Performance reporting for each SBU measures financial responsibility. SBUs are often subdivided into additional categories, including product lines, geographic areas, or customers. Specific SBU classifications include:

5.1   Cost SBU

Managers are held responsible for controlling costs in a cost SBU.

5.2   Revenue SBU

Managers are held responsible for generating revenues in a revenue SBU.

5.3   Profit SBU

Managers are held responsible for producing a target profit (i.e., accountability for both revenue and costs) in a profit SBU.

5.4   Investment SBU

Managers are held responsible for the return on the assets invested in an investment SBU. The return must be equal to or greater than the management's minimum required rate of return.

Question 5-1   FR-00174

Elmhurst Corporation is considering changes to its responsibility accounting system. Which of the following statements is/are correct for a responsibility accounting system?

I.   In a cost SBU, managers are responsible for controlling costs but not revenue.

II. The idea behind responsibility accounting is that a manager should be held responsible for those items, and only those items, that the manager can actually control to a significant extent.

III. To be effective, a good responsibility accounting system must provide for both planning and control. Planning without control and control without planning is not effective.

IV. Common costs that are allocated to a SBU are normally controllable by the SBU's management.

    1. I and II only are correct.

    2. II and III only are correct.

    3. I, II, and III are correct.

    4. I, II, and IV are correct.

---

6 Balanced Scorecards

The balanced scorecard (generally a senior management or executive tool) is a control mechanism that gathers information on multiple dimensions of an organization's performance defined by critical success factors necessary to accomplish firm strategy. Critical success factors can be classified within various categories and are commonly displayed as:

6.1 Financial Performance

This category includes critical financial performance measures, such as the current ratio or gross margin.

6.2 Internal Business Processes

This category includes critical business process measures, such as through-put time.

6.3 Customer Satisfaction

This category includes critical customer satisfaction measures, such as customer retention.

6.4 Advancement of Innovation and Human Resource Development

This category includes critical learning and growth measures, such as employee retention, innovations, suggestions made and accepted, etc.

Question 6-1   FR-00184

Canarsie Corporation uses a balanced scorecard to evaluate its digital camera manufacturing operation. Which of the following statements with respect to balanced scorecards is/are correct?

I. A balanced scorecard reports management information regarding organizational performance in achieving goals classified by critical success factors to demonstrate that no single dimension of organizational performance can be relied upon to evaluate success.

II. Performance measures used in a balanced scorecard tend to be divided into financial, customer, internal business process, and learning and growth.

III. In a balanced scorecard, internal business processes are what the company does in its attempts to satisfy customers.

   1. I and II only are correct.
   2. II and III only are correct.
   3. III only is correct.
   4. I, II, and III are correct.

---

1 Absorption (Full) vs. Variable (Direct) Costing

The absorption costing method is a U.S. GAAP basis calculation of gross profit, while variable costing develops contribution margins compatible with breakeven analysis. Variable costing is not allowed for financial reporting purposes under U.S. GAAP.

1.1 Assumptions

General assumptions of cost-volume-profit (CVP) analysis include:

- Costs are either variable or fixed, with volume the only relevant factor affecting cost.
- In relation to production volume, all costs behave in a linear fashion.
- Over the relevant range of production volume, cost behaviors will remain constant.
- The longer (shorter) the time period, the greater the percentage of variable (fixed) costs.

1.2 Absorption (Full Costing) Approach

Absorption costing capitalizes fixed factory overhead as part of inventory in accordance with GAAP. Therefore, absorption costing includes direct materials, direct labor, and fixed and variable overhead.

Revenue	XXX
Less: Cost of goods sold	(XXX)
Gross profit	XXX
Less: Operating expenses	(XXX)
Net income	XXX

1.3 Variable (Direct Costing) Approach

In variable (direct) costing, only variable manufacturing costs (direct materials, direct labor, and variable factory overhead) are included in inventory. Fixed factory overhead is excluded from inventory and treated as a period cost:

Sales	XXX
Less: Variable costs	(XXX)
Contribution margin	XXX
Less: Fixed costs	(XXX)
Net income	XXX

1.4   Income Effect

Relationship Between Production and Sales for the Period	Effect on Inventories	Relationship Between Absorption and Variable Costing Net Incomes
Production = Sales	No change in inventories	Absorption costing net income = Variable costing net income
Production > Sales	Inventory increase	Absorption costing net income* > Variable costing net income
Production < Sales	Inventory decrease	Absorption costing net income** < Variable costing net income

*   Net income is higher under absorption costing because fixed manufacturing overhead cost is deferred in inventory as inventories increase.

**   Net income is lower under absorption costing because fixed manufacturing overhead cost is released from inventory as inventories decrease.

Question 1-1   FR-00261

Omni Inc. planned and actually manufactured 200,000 units of its single product in its first year of operation. Variable manufacturing costs were $30 per unit of product. Planned and actual fixed manufacturing costs were $600,000, and selling and administrative costs totaled $400,000 in Year 1. Omni sold 120,000 units of product in Year 1 at a selling price of $40 per unit.

Omni's Year 1 operating income using variable costing is:

     1. $200,000

     2. $440,000

     3. $800,000

     4. $600,000

?   Related Questions

For related questions, go to the online question bank:

➤   FR-00133

➤   FR-00153

➤   FR-00172

➤   FR-00239

➤   FR-00257

➤   FR-00276

➤   FR-00278

➤   FR-00280

2 Breakeven Analysis

Breakeven analysis determines the sales required (in dollars or units) to result in zero profit or loss from operations. After breakeven has been achieved, each additional unit sold will increase net income by the amount of the contribution margin per unit.

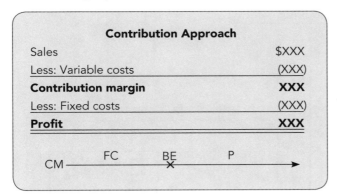

2.1 Standard Formulas

2.1.1 Breakeven Point in Units

$$\frac{\text{Total fixed costs}}{\text{Contribution margin per unit}} = \text{Breakeven point in units}$$

2.1.2 Breakeven Point in Dollars

■ Multiply the selling price per unit by the breakeven units:

$$\text{Unit price} \times \text{Breakeven point in units} = \text{Breakeven point in dollars}$$

■ Contribution margin ratio approach:

$$\frac{\text{Total fixed costs}}{\text{Contribution margin ratio*}} = \text{Breakeven point in dollars}$$

* Contribution margin ratio = Contribution margin/Sales

2.2 Required Sales for a Desired Profit

Breakeven analysis can be extended to calculate the required sales to produce a desired pretax income by treating the desired profit as another fixed cost.

2.2.1 Required Sales in Units

$$\text{Required sales (units)} = \frac{\text{Total fixed cost } + \text{ Desired profit}}{\text{C/M per unit}}$$

2.2.2 Required Sales in Dollars

$$\text{Required sales (\$)} = \frac{\text{Total fixed cost } + \text{ Desired profit}}{\text{C/M \%}}$$

2.3 Breakeven Chart

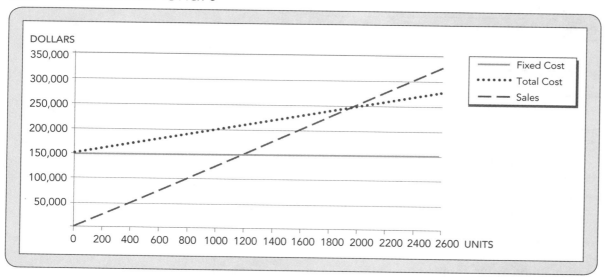

2.4 Margin of Safety

The margin of safety is the excess of sales over breakeven sales.

■ The margin of safety expressed in dollars is calculated as follows:

> Total sales in dollars − Breakeven sales in dollars = Margin of safety in dollars

■ The margin of safety can also be expressed as a percentage of sales:

$$\frac{\text{Margin of safety in dollars}}{\text{Total sales}} = \text{Margin of safety percentage}$$

2.5 Target Costing

Target costing is used to establish the product cost allowed that ensures both total sales volume and profitability per unit. With target pricing, the selling price of the product will determine the production costs allowed. The target cost will be equal to the market price less the required profit.

Question 2-1   FR-00163

Lampassas Corporation manufactures product Lam at its manufacturing facility. At annual sales of $900,000 for Year 1, product Lam had the following unit sales price and costs:

Sales price	$20
Prime cost	6
Manufacturing overhead	
Variable	1
Fixed	7
Selling & administrative costs	
Variable	1
Fixed	3
	18
Profit	$ 2

What was product Lam's breakeven point in dollars?

1. $500,000
2. $750,000
3. $630,000
4. $900,000

? Related Questions

For related questions, go to the online question bank:

➤ FR-00173

➤ FR-00182

3 Transfer Pricing

3.1 Non-Global Perspective

A transfer price is the price charged for the sale/purchase of a product internally (between two divisions within one overall company). Prices are set based on the following strategies: negotiated price, market price, and cost.

3.2 Global Perspective

Transfer pricing is a methodology for allocating profits or losses among related entities within the same corporation (or legal group) in different tax jurisdictions. Transfer prices should approximate the prices for comparable transactions between unrelated parties. Comparability may be assessed using the following strategies:

1. Transactional methods (comparable uncontrolled price, resale price, gross margin, cost plus).

2. Profitability methods (comparable profits, transactional net margin, comparable profit split, residual profit split).

4 Special Orders

Special order decisions are defined as generally infrequent opportunities that require the firm to decide if a special order should be accepted or rejected. Generally, most direct and variable costs are considered as well as incremental costs.

4.1 Presumed Excess Capacity

- Compare the incremental (additional) costs of the order to the incremental (additional) revenue generated by the order. This process compares the variable cost per unit to the revenue generated per unit.

- Provided the selling price per unit is greater than the variable cost per unit, the contribution margin will increase and the special order should be accepted.

- Fixed costs are sunk and will not be relevant to these decisions.

4.2 Presumed Full Capacity

- Extend the analysis described above to include opportunity cost.

- The opportunity cost will be the contribution margin that would have been produced if the special order were not accepted.

- The production that is forfeited to produce the special order is referred to as the next best alternative use of the facility.

5 Make or Buy Decisions

Similar to accepting or rejecting a special order, managers must consider capacity and, where appropriate, opportunity costs.

5.1   Excess Capacity

If there is excess capacity, the cost of making the product internally is the cost that will be avoided (or saved) if the product is not made. This will be the maximum outside purchase price. Compare variable costs to the purchase price and select the cheapest alternative.

5.2   No Excess Capacity

If there is no excess capacity, the cost of making the product internally is the cost that will be avoided (saved) if the product is not made plus the opportunity cost associated with the decision. Compare the variable costs plus opportunity cost to the purchase price and select the cheapest alternative.

5.3   First Use Existing Capacity Efficiently

Make-or-buy decisions attempt to use existing capacity as efficiently as possible before purchasing from an outside supplier.

Question 5-1   FR-00291

The Harbor Company currently makes 10,000 bolts a year for $50,000. The Cove Corporation has offered to sell Harbor the bolts for $4.00 a piece. Harbor has the cost structure shown below:

	Total	Per Unit
Direct Material	$ 5,000	$0.50
Direct Labor	15,000	1.50
Variable factory overhead	10,000	1.00
Fixed factory overhead	20,000	2.00
Total	$50,000	$5.00

Upon further analysis, Harbor notes that the company can eliminate the services of a $15,000 per year supervisor accounted for in fixed factory overhead if they elect to buy. Harbor's decision to make or buy would result in a comparison of the purchase price of $4.00 to a production cost of:

1. $2.00
2. $3.00
3. $4.50
4. $5.00

Related Questions

For related questions, go to the online question bank:

➤ FR-00289

Forecasting and Projection

6 Sell or Process Further

Management's decision as to whether to sell at the split-off point involves comparing the incremental revenues and incremental costs generated after the split-off point. Separable costs (incurred after split-off) are relevant, while joint costs (incurred prior to split-off) are not relevant.

- ■ **Sell:** Incremental costs > Incremental revenues.
- ■ **Process Further:** Incremental revenues > Incremental costs.

7 Keep or Drop a Segment

The decision to keep or drop a segment involves comparing the lost contribution margin to avoidable fixed costs if the segment is dropped. Avoidable fixed costs go away if the segment is dropped and are therefore relevant. Unavoidable fixed costs will be reallocated to other products and continue to be incurred by the company even if the segment is dropped, therefore making them irrelevant.

- ■ **Keep:** Lost contribution margin > Avoidable fixed costs.
- ■ **Drop:** Avoidable fixed costs >   Lost contribution margin.

8 Regression Analysis

Linear regression is a method for studying the relationship between two or more variables. Using regression analysis, variation in the dependent variable is explained using one or more independent variables. The dependent variable is specified to be a linear function of one or more independent variables.

8.1 Simple Linear Regression vs. Multiple Linear Regression Analysis

Simple regression involves only one independent variable. Multiple regression analysis involves more than one independent variable. The simple linear regression model takes the following form:

$$y = a + bx$$
$$\text{Total cost} = \text{Fixed cost} + \text{Variable rate (units)}$$

E-8   **V**   *Business Final Review*

© Becker Professional Education Corporation. All rights reserved.

Question 8-1   FR-00277

The primary difference between simple linear regression and multiple linear regression is:

1. Multiple linear regression analysis involves more that one independent variable while simple linear regression only considers one independent variable.

2. Multiple linear regression analysis considers the impact of one independent variable on multiple dependent variables while simple linear regression analysis only considers one dependent variable.

3. Multiple linear regression analysis considers the impact of multiple independent variables on multiple dependent variables while simple linear regression analysis only considers one independent and one dependent variable.

4. Multiple linear regression analysis considers codependent variables while simple linear regression analysis only considers mutually exclusive variables.

---

9 Statistical Measures Used to Evaluate Regression Analysis

9.1 Coefficient of Correlation (r)

The coefficient of correlation measures the strength of the linear relationship between the independent variable (x) and the dependent variable (y). In standard notation, the coefficient of correlation is r. The range of r is from -1.0 to $+1.0$, with a value of -1.0 indicating a perfect negative correlation and a value of 1.0 indicating a perfect positive correlation.

9.2 Coefficient of Determination (R^2)

The coefficient of determination (R^2) may be interpreted as the portion of the total variation in the dependent variable (y) explained by the independent variable (x). Its value lies between zero and one. The higher the R^2, the greater the proportion of the total variation in y that is explained by the variation in x. That is, the higher the R^2, the better the fit of the regression line.

Question 9-1   FR-00214

Ivey Company uses regression analysis in examining its costs. It has determined that there is a correlation coefficient of 0.90 between two variables X and Y. Which of the following statements is correct for a correlation coefficient of 0.90?

1. There is little relationship between X and Y.

2. Variation in X explains 90% of the variation in Y.

3. If X increases, Y will never decrease.

4. If X increases, Y will generally increase.

? Related Questions

For related questions, go to the online question bank:

➤ FR-00279

10 Learning Curve Analysis

Learning curve analysis is based on the idea that per-unit labor hours will decline as workers become more familiar with a specific task or production process.

Example

If workers take 30 hours to produce the first unit of a product, and 18 hours to produce the second unit, the learning curve rate will be 80% [(30+18)/(30+30)] and the average time per unit will be 24 hours.

11 High-Low Method

The high-low point method is used to estimate the fixed and variable portions of cost. It assumes that the differences between costs at the highest and lowest production levels are due directly to variable costs. Variable and fixed costs are calculated as follows:

11.1   Computation of Variable Cost per Unit

$$\frac{\text{Costs at high } - \text{ Costs at low}}{\text{Activities at high } - \text{ Activities at low}} = \frac{\text{Changes in costs}}{\text{Changes in activities}} = \text{Variable cost per unit}$$

11.2 Computation of Total Fixed Costs

Total cost − (Variable cost per unit × Activity) = Fixed costs

Question 11-1   FR-00143

Presented below is the production data for the first eight months of the year for the mixed costs incurred by Mouton Corporation:

Month	Cost	Units
January	$14,700	1,800
February	15,200	1,900
March	13,700	1,700
April	14,000	1,600
May	14,300	1,500
June	13,100	1,300
July	12,800	1,100
August	14,600	1,500

Mouton Corporation uses the high-low method to analyze mixed costs. Variable cost per unit and fixed cost are respectively:

	VC	FC
1.	$1.00	$13,100
2.	$3.00	$9,500
3.	$1.00	$12,800
4.	$2.00	$15,200

Class Question Explanations

Topic A

QUESTION 2-1

Choice "1" is correct.

An audit committee member may qualify for classification as a financial expert using most any combination of education or experience auditing or preparing financial reports. The member must understand generally accepted accounting principles and how to apply them and understand internal control.

Choice "2" is incorrect. There is no requirement that the audit committee financial expert meet minimum service requirements on the board of directors.

Choice "3" is incorrect. Although the audit committee member qualifying as its financial expert may have technical training and experience as an auditor, that is not a requirement. The audit committee member may qualify under any number of different means.

Choice "4" is incorrect. Disclosure of the financial expert is required.

QUESTION 3-1

Choice "3" is correct.

Risk response is a separate component of the COSO *Enterprise Risk Management—Integrated Framework*, not the *Internal Control—Integrated Framework*.

Choice "1" is incorrect. Control environment is known as the tone at the top and is one of the five components of the COSO *Internal Control—Integrated Framework*.

Choice "2" is incorrect. Risk assessment is one of the five components of the COSO *Internal Control—Integrated Framework*.

Choice "4" is incorrect. Control activities generally describes control policies and procedures and is one of the five components of the COSO *Internal Control—Integrated Framework*.

QUESTION 4-1

Choice "2" is correct.

ERM anticipates the development of strategies that are aligned with individual risk appetites and the willingness to accept risk.

Choice "1" is incorrect. All risk cannot be avoided. Risk avoidance is only one of five responses to risk, which also include reduction, sharing, acceptance, and pursuit.

Choice "3" is incorrect. ERM considers business objectives at all layers of the organization, not purely strategy at the entity level.

Choice "4" is incorrect. Uncertainty can rarely be eliminated. ERM can only help reduce uncertainty.

Business II

Topic A

QUESTION 1-1   FR-00137

Choice "3" is correct.

Nominal GDP measures the value of goods and services in current dollars, while real GDP measures the value of goods and services in constant dollars. Real GDP is calculated as:

$$\text{Real GDP} = \frac{\text{Nominal GDP}}{\text{GDP Deflator}} \times 100$$

Thus, from the values for the GDP deflator and nominal GDP given in the problem, we have:

$$\text{Real GDP} = \frac{\$10,000 \text{ billion}}{125} \times 100 = \$8,000 \text{ billion}$$

QUESTION 2-1   FR-00157

Choice "1" is correct.

The labor force includes all individuals 16 years of age or older who are either working or actively seeking work. To be in the labor force, a person must be actively seeking employment. Thus, the 100 individuals who gave up looking for work are not in the labor force. Similarly, the 100 individuals who are under the age of 16 or retired are not in the labor force. The total labor force is therefore 800: the 600 individuals who hold jobs and the 200 individuals looking for jobs. The unemployment rate is the ratio of the number of unemployed individuals to the total labor force. Because individuals who have given up looking for work are not classified as unemployed, the unemployment rate is 200/800 = 0.25 or 25%.

QUESTION 2-2   FR-00207

Choice "4" is correct.

Fiscal policy refers to government spending and tax policies. Expansionary fiscal policy consists of increases in government spending and/or decreases in taxes. When the government increases government spending and/or decreases taxes, the aggregate demand curve shifts right. As a result, real GDP increases leading to an increase in, or expansion of, economic activity.

Topic B

QUESTION 1-1   FR-00259

Choice "4" is correct.

A reduction in the personal income tax will cause an increase in aggregate demand (i.e., a shift in the aggregate demand curve to the right). As a result, a reduction in taxes will cause unemployment to fall and real GDP to rise.

Choice "1" is incorrect. Real GDP would rise, not fall.

Choice "2" is incorrect. Unemployment will fall, not rise.

Choice "3" is incorrect. The opposite will occur; unemployment will fall and real GDP will rise.

Business II

QUESTION 3-1   FR-00128

Choice "2" is correct.

An increase in production costs shifts the supply curve to the left. As a result, equilibrium price will rise and equilibrium quantity will fall.

Choice "1" is incorrect because an increase in consumer income would shift the demand curve to the right causing equilibrium quantity to rise.

Choice "3" is incorrect because an increase in the price of a substitute good would shift the demand curve to the right causing equilibrium quantity to rise.

Choice "4" is incorrect since a decrease in the price of a complementary good would shift demand to the right causing equilibrium quantity to rise.

QUESTION 3-2   FR-00241

Choice "3" is correct.

When the supply curve shifts to the left, equilibrium price will rise and equilibrium quantity will fall.

Choice "1" is incorrect. Equilibrium price and quantity will increase when the demand curve shifts to the right.

Choice "2" is incorrect. Equilibrium price and quantity will fall when the demand curve shifts to the left.

Choice "4" is incorrect. Equilibrium price will fall and equilibrium quantity will rise when the supply curve shifts to the right.

QUESTION 4-1   FR-00138

Choice "3" is correct.

The price elasticity of demand is defined as:

$$\text{Price elasticity of demand Real GDP} = \frac{\% \text{ Change in quantity demanded}}{\% \text{ Change in price}}$$

Using the point method of calculating price elasticity of demand, if the price of a product rises from $5 to $6 and the demand for that product decreases from 100 pounds to 90 pounds, the price elasticity of demand is calculated as follows:

$$\frac{\% \text{ Change in quantity demanded}}{\% \text{ Change in price}} = \frac{(90 - 100) \,/\, 100}{(\$6 - \$5) \,/\, \$5} = \frac{(0.10)}{0.20} = (0.50)$$

Choices "1", "2", and "4" are incorrect per the above explanation.

QUESTION 6-1   FR-00158

Choice "4" is correct.

A perfectly competitive market is characterized by: (1) a large number of firms, (2) very little product differentiation (firms sell identical products), and (3) no barriers to market entry.

Choice "1" is incorrect because firms in a perfectly competitive market sell a homogeneous product and, thus, don't compete via product differentiation.

Choice "2" is incorrect by definition. A perfectly competitive market has no barriers to entry.

Choice "3" is incorrect because it describes oligopoly.

Business II

QUESTION 7-1

FR-00247

Choice "4" is correct.

Strategy is generally influenced by four factors, divided between internal and external factors. Internal factors include an individual firm's strengths and weaknesses, while external factors include opportunities and threats. The discovery of a microbe in the environment that impacts sales is a threat.

Choice "1" is incorrect. Clearly, an external event that reduces sales is not a strength.

Choice "2" is incorrect. The discovery of an external challenge that reduces revenue is a threat, not a weakness.

Choice "3" is incorrect. An external event, as described, that decreases sales is not an opportunity.

QUESTION 7-2

FR-00228

Choice "1" is correct.

In this question, they want to know which of a series of statements with respect to competitive strategies is/are (more than likely) correct. "All of the above" is available if all of the statements are correct.

Statement I says that cost leadership strategies typically focus on building market share and matching the prices of rival firms and that a possible reason for the lack of success of Rivington's cost leadership strategy is that it has an outmoded warehousing and distribution system. Cost leadership strategies certainly focus on building market share and matching prices, and an outmoded warehousing and distribution system could certainly keep a firm from reducing its costs sufficiently. Statement I is correct.

Statement II says that differentiation strategies attempt to gain competitive advantage by creating the perception that products are superior to those of competitors and that a reason for the lack of success of Rivington's differentiation strategy is that it implemented its strategy by advertising its "everyday low prices." The definition of differentiation strategies is correct. However, "everyday low prices" is not normally a way to implement a differentiation strategy, and that could have been a reason for the lack of success of the strategy. Statement II is correct.

Statement III says that vertical integration strategies attempt to control an entire supply chain and that a possible reason for the lack of success of Rivington's strategy is that it had not acquired any of the companies in its supply chain. Acquiring companies is not a necessary factor for the control of a supply chain. Statement III is incorrect.

QUESTION 8-1

FR-00178

Choice "4" is correct.

In this question, they want to know which, if any, of a series of statements with respect to value chain analysis is/are correct. "None of the above" is available if none of the statements is correct.

Statement I says that value chain analysis is a tool used by companies to assess the perceived value of a company by potential stockholders. Actually, value chain analysis is a tool used to assess the perceived value of a company by its customers, who might or might not be potential stockholders. Statement I is incorrect.

Statement II says that value chain analysis starts with an identification of cost drivers and ends with the development of means of obtaining competitive advantage. Before the cost drivers can be identified, however, the value chain activities must be identified. The cost drivers associated with each activity are then identified. Statement II is incorrect.

Statement III says that types of value chain analysis are internal cost analysis, internal differentiation analysis, and vertical linkage analysis, all of which examine internal costs to determine perceived value and competitive advantage. Internal cost analysis and internal (product) differentiation analysis certainly examine internal costs and value, but vertical linkage analysis looks outside the firm at the suppliers and purchasers of the products. Statement III is incorrect.

Business II

Topic C

QUESTION 1-1   FR-00269

Choice "3" is correct.

Credit risk relates to a debtor's exposure to either the inability to secure financing or the inability to secure financing at attractive interest rates. Arbor's use of long-term financing locks in financing at predictable rates and is designed to eliminate risk that credit might not be available.

Choice "1" is incorrect. Interest rate risk generally relates to the changes in valuation of investments that result from interest rate fluctuations. Although Arbor Corporation is concerned about changes in interest rates, its concern relates to meeting ongoing credit needs, not the valuation of its instrument.

Choice "2" is incorrect. Market risk relates to nondiversifiable risks associated with participation in the economy. Although the Arbor Corporation is concerned about its appeal in the market place as a borrower, its predominant concern relates to its company-specific business risks that might impede the ability to secure credit to meet ongoing working capital needs.

Choice "4" is incorrect. Default risk represents a creditor's exposure to non-payment. The question relates to the debtor's risk exposure.

QUESTION 2-1   FR-00826

Choice "4" is correct.

The minimum annual percentage earned by an investment that will cause a company to put money into a particular security or project.

The required rate of return is the risk-free rate plus the financial risks that represent possible exposure to loss plus an inflation premium. Market risk is the possible loss in trading value of assets or liabilities in markets, due to the overall performance of the market. Market risk is nondiversifiable. Liquidity risk is the risk of a lack of marketability of an investment that cannot be bought or sold quickly enough to prevent or minimize a loss. Default risk is the possibility that a debtor may not repay the principal or interest due on a timely basis. Inflation premium is the rate inflation for the period, an external economic force that the company cannot control. However, inflation reduces the real return of an investment, so it must be added back to the required rate.

Choices "1", "2", and "3" are incorrect, based on the above explanation.

QUESTION 4-1   FR-00236

Choice "4" is correct.

The question asks which of the answer options would NOT serve to improve the exchange rate of the U.S. dollar relative to foreign currencies.

Choice "4" is correct because increased United States capital investment in a foreign economy would likely cause the exchange rate for the United States dollar to deteriorate. Increased capital investment in a foreign country creates a demand for the foreign currency. The increased demand for a fixed amount of foreign currency ultimately increases the value (exchange rate) of the foreign currency relative to the United States dollar.

Choice "1" is incorrect because foreign inflation would reduce the buying power of the foreign currency, thereby increasing the value of the United States dollar, which caused the exchange rate to improve.

Choice "2" is incorrect because declining domestic income will reduce the amount of domestic currency spent. Reduced demand for foreign currency from a declining pool of domestic currency will effectively strengthen the domestic currency and improve exchange rates.

Choice "3" is incorrect because low foreign interest rates will reduce incentives for foreign investment. The less demand for foreign currency, the stronger the domestic currency. Exchange rates improve.

QUESTION 5-1   FR-00242

Choice "2" is correct.

Approach: Set up assumed values for transactions and test for appropriate gain or loss.

Receivable

Denominated in yen. Assume the transaction is for 1,000 yen. On the settlement date, there is a foreign exchange gain on the receipt of 1,000 yen. In order for there to be a gain, the 1,000 yen must be worth more dollars than on the transaction date. Therefore, fewer yen must be equal to a dollar (for there to be more dollars), so the number of yen exchangeable into dollars decreased.

Payable

Denominated in euros. Assume the transaction is for 2,000 euros. On the settlement date, there is a foreign exchange loss on the payment of 2,000 euros. For there to be a loss, it must take more dollars to buy the same euros. Therefore, the number of euros exchangeable into dollars must have decreased.

QUESTION 5-2   FR-00198

Choice "2" is correct.

The question asks which of the series of items describes Hickman International's exposure to economic risks of exchange rate fluctuation.

Economic exposure represents the potential that the present value of an organization's cash flows could increase or decrease as a result of changes in the exchange rate. Economic exposure is generally defined through local currency appreciation or depreciation and measured in relation to the organization's earnings and cash flows.

This choice is correct because net inflows of a depreciated local currency (Canadian dollar) relative to a domestic currency (United States dollar) results in economic loss.

Choice "1" is incorrect because it represents a transaction risk.

Choices "3" and "4" are incorrect because they represent translation risks.

Business II

Choice "1" is correct.

The question asks which financial instrument would be used by Siaggas International to hedge amounts it owes on individual accounts payable that are denominated in euros.

Futures contracts for foreign currency represent the obligation to buy or sell a particular number of foreign currency units at a specific time and at a specific date. Futures contracts are often used to hedge specific contracts, while forward contracts are used to specify general foreign currency needs. Hedge contracts to mitigate risks associated with liabilities are call or buy contracts. The company locks in the amount of foreign currency it needs to satisfy its obligation ensuring that a weakening domestic currency won't make the settlement more expensive.

Choice "2" is incorrect because a futures contract to sell would be applicable to accounts receivable.

Choices "3" and "4" are incorrect because forward contracts would normally not be used in this situation.

Therefore, the correct answer is choice "1". Futures contracts to buy euros would be used to hedge transaction exposure to exchange rate risk for an account payable.

Topic A

QUESTION 2-1   FR-00221

Choice "1" is correct.

Letters of credit are third-party guarantees of obligations incurred by Cash Burn Enterprises. The letter of credit would provide specific assurances to otherwise unsecured creditors that payment is assured, thereby ensuring their consistent cooperation to provide needed supplies.

Choice "2" is incorrect. Lines of credit provide a defined safety net for cash availability, but provide comparatively less assurances that cash flows would be dedicated to specific vendors. A letter of credit (vs. a line of credit) meets the objective of providing specific assurances to vendors.

Choice "3" is incorrect. Subordinated debentures are higher-risk (higher yield) securities that potentially provide cash infusion, but provide comparatively less assurances that cash flows would be dedicated to specific vendors.

Choice "4" is incorrect. Working capital financing is nothing more than using the period allowed by trade creditors to spontaneously finance short-term purchases. Working capital financing is potentially dangerous in circumstances where receipts may lag behind disbursement obligations. Nonpayment can result in default and interruption of supplies. Cash Burn Enterprises would not use this strategy.

QUESTION 5-1   FR-00816

Choice "2" is correct.

Investors and firms both use leverage—operating and financial leverage—in an effort to generate higher profits. However, the use of leverage will magnify losses as well as profits. High operating leverage stems from the use of a high percentage of fixed costs relative to variable costs. Once sales have covered the fixed costs, additional sales (and lower variable costs) will result in higher operating income. The opposite is true for losses; higher operating leverage magnifies losses because the fixed costs still have to be covered even when sales decline. A similar situation occurs with financial leverage, which stems from a higher percentage of debt, rather than equity, financing. Once sales are sufficient to cover the fixed interest payments, additional sales (less variable expenses) will result in higher operating income, which would be available as returns to equity holders.

Choice "1" is incorrect. Financing the firm with a high percentage of long-term debt results in financial leverage. The relative proportion of debt versus equity financing does not affect operating leverage. Operating leverage results from a high percentage of fixed operating costs.

Choice "3" is correct. Using a high degree of both types of leverage increases risk, based on the need to cover the high fixed costs. With the higher risk, you may have higher returns or you may have higher losses, depending on the operating results.

Choice "4" is incorrect. Increasing variable operating expenses decreases operating leverage and does not affect financial leverage. Operating leverage is higher when fixed costs are higher. Financial leverage is higher when the firm uses a higher percentage of long-term debt to finance the operations.

Business Final Review

Business III

Choice "2" is correct.

The cost of preferred stock is computed as using the formula below with the terms defined below:

$$Kps = Dps / Nps$$

Dps = Cash dividends on preferred stock (1,000 shares × $50 × 8%)		$ 4,000
Nps = Proceeds of preferred stock sale net of fees and costs		
Proceeds (1,000 shares × $52)	$52,000	
Flotation costs	(2,500)	
Net proceeds (Nps)		$49,500
Cost of capital ($4,000 / $49,500)		8.08%

Choice "1" is incorrect. The cost of capital is computed as the dividend amount divided by the net proceeds (computed as the total amount collected from the sale of the stock issue net of flotation costs, not the par value, net of flotation costs).

Choice "3" is incorrect. The cost of capital is not the stated rate of the issue.

Choice "4" is incorrect. The cost of capital is computed as the dividend amount divided by the net proceeds (computed as the total amount collected from the sale of the stock issue net of flotation costs, not market proceeds prior to consideration of flotation costs).

Choice "3" is correct.

The capital asset pricing model for computation of the cost of equity financing (retained earnings) uses the formula below with terms defined as follows:

kre = krf + [bi × (km − krf)]	
krf = risk-free rate of return	2.00%
bi = beta coefficient of stock (1.25 / 1.00)	1.25
km = market rate	12.00%
km − krf = market risk premium (12% − 2%)	10.00%
kre = 2% + [1.25 × (12% − 2%)]	
kre = 2% + [1.25 × 10%]	
kre = 2% + [12.50%]	
kre = 14.5%	

Choice "1" is incorrect. The cost of equity capital is not the risk-free rate of return.

Choice "2" is incorrect. The cost of equity capital is not the expected return on the market.

Choice "4" is incorrect. The cost of equity capital is not the market risk premium.

Topic B

QUESTION 3-1

Choice "1" is correct.

Compensating balance arrangements are a mechanism to reduce fees, not to increase the availability of cash. Compensating balances normally decrease the availability of cash since they represent an agreement to maintain a minimum balance in exchange for reduced fees.

Choice "2" is incorrect. Zero-balance accounts are designed to increase the availability of cash. Banking arrangements are made to assume a theoretical zero balance in a particular account and to replenish the account when checks are presented. Maintaining a zero balance in an operating account ensures that cash is invested for the maximum period before disbursement.

Choice "3" is incorrect. Electronic funds transfers expedite deposits. Funds are electronically transferred for deposit without waiting for mail delivery and manual deposit processing by the recipient and the bank.

Choice "4" is incorrect. Lock box systems increase the availability of cash by expediting deposits. Receipts are sent directly to a dedicated mailing address and processed immediately by the bank, thereby skipping the internal deposit processing procedures of the recipient.

QUESTION 4-1

Choice "3" is correct.

Computing the annual interest rate associated with cash discounts is developed as follows:

1. Compute the annualized increment for the discount:
   Days per year ÷ Days outstanding after discount
   360 ÷ (30 − 12) = 20

2. Compute the effective interest rate with discount:
   2% ÷ (100% − 2%) = 2.048%

3. Multiply the annualized increment by the rate:
   2.048% × 20 = 40.8%

Choice "1" is incorrect. Multiplying 2% by 12 months provides the answer of 24% is incorrect per above.

Choice "2" is incorrect. The annualized interest rate for 2/10 net 30 terms is 36.7%. Although these terms are common, the annualized results are not universal.

Choice "4" is incorrect. This response computes the annualized increment for the discount based upon the days during which the discount is effective (12) vs. the days outstanding after the discount (18).

Business III

Choice "2" is correct.

Average collection period is the result of two formulas:

1. **Receivable turnover**

Net Sales	$730,000
Average receivables (47,000 + 41,000) / 2	÷ 44,000
Receivable turnover	16.59

2. **Average collection period**

Days per year	365
Receivable turnover	÷ 16.59
Average collection period	22.00

Choice "1" is incorrect. The receivable turnover is a component of the average collection period computation.

Choice "3" is incorrect. Average collection period is the days in the year divided by the receivable turnover ratio. The receivable turnover is annual sales divided by average receivables, not average sales divided by average receivables as suggested by this answer.

Choice "4" is incorrect. The receivable turnover is annual sales divided by average receivables, not sales divided by year-end receivables as suggested by this answer.

Choice "1" is correct.

The optimal inventory order is formulated by the economic order quantity equation shown below with the following term definitions:

EOQ	=	Economic order quantity	
S	=	Annual sales in units	2,500
O	=	Cost per purchase order	$ 1,000
C	=	Carrying cost per unit	$ 500

$$EOQ = \sqrt{\frac{2SO}{C}}$$

$$EOQ = \sqrt{\frac{2(2,500 \times \$1,000)}{\$500}}$$

$$EOQ = 100$$

Choice "2" is incorrect. The economic order quantity is not equal to the stock-out costs divided by the months of the year. Stock-out costs are irrelevant to economic order quantity.

Choice "3" is incorrect. The economic order quantity is not equal to sales in units divided by the months in the year.

Choice "4" is incorrect. The economic order quantity is not equal to double the stock-out costs divided by the months in the year. Stock-out costs are irrelevant to economic order quantity.

Topic C

QUESTION 7-1   FR-00827

Choice "4" is correct.

This choice is not an influence on subjective assumptions. Instead, it is an assumption underlying the Black-Scholes method of valuing options.

Choice "1" is incorrect. Generalized rules of thumb are influences on subjective assumptions. Use of rules of thumb is normally considered to be "intuition" rather than objective analysis, a guideline that provides simplified advice regarding a particular subject. Rules of thumb develop as a result of experience rather than theory. An example of a rule of thumb is "always have three to six months of expenses in an emergency fund."

Choice "2" is incorrect. Behavior biases are influences on subjective assumptions. These are usually based on the personality characteristics of the analyst, and also include confirmation bias and illusion of control. Confirmation bias occurs when people filter out potentially useful facts and opinions that do not coincide with their preconceived notions. This causes them to overlook information that disagrees with their own opinions, which could result in poor decisions. Illusion of control occurs when people overestimate their ability to control events over which they really have no actual control.

Choice "3" is incorrect. The effect of loss aversion is an influence on subjective assumptions. This is the tendency to strongly prefer avoiding losses over acquiring gains. According to economics and decision theory, human beings would rather not lose a dollar than to gain a dollar. This leads to loss aversion in decision making, which may not always yield the best result.

QUESTION 7-2   FR-00231

Choice "2" is correct.

Business losses are generally deemed to be the most emotionally distracting influence on decision makers. The manager's fear of continued losses and aversion to a sure loss can motivate the manager to continue to operate losing projects for too long and thereby magnify losses.

Choice "1" is incorrect. Overconfidence can distort business decisions, but it can be easily countered with analysis rather than the fear that accompanies losses.

Choice "3" is incorrect. Use of available data, particularly the most easily available data, can be used to confirm judgments rather than rigorously challenge decisions. Additional questioning can resolve this issue and more easily be accomplished than overcoming fear of losses.

Choice "4" is incorrect. Excessive optimism can distort decision making, however, this emotion is more easily countered with analysis than the irrational emotion that often accompanies the fear of losses.

Business III

Topic D

Choice "2" is correct.

After-tax cash flow is computed as the sum of cash inflows (net of tax) plus the depreciation tax shield afforded by depreciation. After-tax cash flows can be computed in one of two ways:

1. Compute the cash flow after tax and add back the depreciation tax shield:

Cash inflow	$150,000	
@ 1 − tax rate	65%	$ 97,500
Depreciation	50,000	
@ tax rate	35%	17,500
After-tax cash flow		$115,000

2. Compute the taxable cash inflow, compute taxes, and reduce cash inflow by the amount of the taxes.

Cash inflow	$150,000
Depreciation	50,000
Taxable cash inflow	100,000
Tax rate	35%
Taxes	35,000

Cash inflow	$150,000
Taxes	35,000
After-tax cash flow	$115,000

Choice "1" is incorrect. This choice computes cash flows net of depreciation without considering tax effects.

Choice "3" is incorrect. This choice erroneously applies a factor equal to 1 − tax rate to the depreciation tax shield in arriving at the after-tax cash flows.

Choice "4" is incorrect. This choice inappropriately discounts the after-tax cash inflows for all five years.

QUESTION 3-1

Choice "4" is correct.

The net present value of an investment is the difference between the present value of the investment and the present value of the after-tax cash flows resulting from the investment. In its most straightforward format, the examiners will give you an even stream of after-tax cash flows and the associated discount factors and require computation of the net present value. In this case, the net present value is computed as follows:

Investment			$(150,000)
After-tax cash flows			
Income	$40,000 × 3.791 =	$151,640	
Salvage	$15,000 × 0.621 =	9,315	
Total after-tax cash flows			160,955
Positive net present value			$ 10,955

Choice "1" is incorrect. The discounted cash flows before salvage are positive, not negative, and the answer does not consider salvage.

Choice "2" is incorrect. The discounted cash flows before salvage are only part of the answer. You must also consider salvage.

Choice "3" is incorrect. The discounted value of the salvage is not the net present value.

Cash flows are after taxes. The tax rate is a distracter.

QUESTION 5-1

Choice "2" is correct.

The payback method is the most simple of all investment evaluation methods. The formula is purely the initial investment divided by the annual cash flows. In this case, the investment is $100,000, and the annual cash flows of $23,850 are used to compute to a payback period of 4.19 years as follows:

$100,000 / $23,850 = 4.19 years

Choice "1" is incorrect. The initial investment is not reduced by the salvage value.

Choice "3" is incorrect. The initial investment is not increased by the salvage value.

Choice "4" is incorrect. This answer is a distracter.

Notes

Business IV

Topic A

QUESTION 1-1 FR-00125

Choice "4" is correct.

Performance measure focuses on putting structure around measuring business performance, and one popular method involves instituting an IT balanced scorecard. The CIO is interested in developing an IT strategy scorecard.

Choice "1" is incorrect. Value delivery focuses on making sure that the IT department does what is necessary to deliver the benefits promised at the beginning of a project or investment. The best way to do this is by developing a process to ensure that certain functions are accelerated when the value proposition is growing, and eliminating functions when the value decreases.

Choice "2" is incorrect. Resource management focuses on managing resources more effectively.

Choice "3" is incorrect. Risk management focuses on instituting a formal risk framework that puts rigor around how IT measures, accepts, and manages risk, as well as reports on what IT is managing in terms of risk.

QUESTION 4-1 FR-00186

Choice "2" is correct.

Top management's most important roles are providing support and encouragement for IT development projects and aligning information systems with corporate strategies. Because business process design often takes time away from other duties, management must ensure that team members are given adequate time and support to work on the project.

Choice "1" is incorrect. Determining information needs and system requirements to communicate to systems developers is the role of the accountant as a user of an accounting information system.

Choice "3" is incorrect. Successful design and implementation of the system is the role of the team members planning each project.

Choice "4" is incorrect. Facilitating the coordination and integration of information systems activities to increase goal congruence and reduce goal conflict is the role of the steering committee.

QUESTION 5-1 FR-00195

Choice "1" is correct.

Under a high-impact category, an organization cannot operate without this information resource for even a short period of time; may experience a high recovery cost; and may realize harm or obstruction to achieving one's mission or to maintaining one's reputation. If Blue Inc. operates with one data center, the information is not backed up in a timely manner, and if a disaster did occur, the company would not be able to operate and would experience a high recovery cost.

Choice "2" is incorrect. Under a medium-impact category, an organization could work around the loss of the information resource for days or perhaps a week but eventually restoration of the resource must occur. In the question, it is stated that Blue cannot operate day-to-day activities without the data center, thus, medium impact would not be the appropriate classification. This also eliminates choice "4".

Choice "3" is incorrect. Under a low-impact category, an organization could operate without this information resource for an extended period of time. In the question, it is stated that Blue cannot operate day-to-day activities without the data center, thus, low impact would not be the appropriate classification. This also eliminates choice "4".

Choice "4" is incorrect. Based on answer choice "2" and "3" explanations, choice "4" is also incorrect.

Business IV

Topic B

QUESTION 1-1   FR-00206

Choice "2" is correct.

Developing a library of key risk indicators to generate different score levels using real-time data analysis tools will allow the major investment bank to monitor the regulatory, compliance, and technology risk areas in real time with transparency.

Choice "1" is incorrect. Descriptive analytics describes events that have already occurred and because the bank wants to monitor key risk areas in real time, this type of analytics is not appropriate.

Choice "3" is incorrect. Predictive analytics uses statistical techniques and forecasting models to predict what could happen. The bank wants to monitor the key risk areas, not predict what could happen.

Choice "4" is incorrect. Analyzing customer demographics and spending patterns with a deal optimization engine does not help the investment bank monitor key risk areas.

QUESTION 2-1   FR-00226

Choice "1" is correct.

A decision support system is a computer-based information system that provides interactive support for managers during the decision-making process. A system that evaluates geophysical and historical data as part of a decision to invest in drilling operations is a decision support system.

Choice "2" is incorrect. A transaction processing system is a system that processes and records routine daily transactions such as cash receipts and disbursements. A system of the character described for drilling sites is normally relatively infrequently run (only as often as there are drilling sites to analyze) and would not meet the definition of a transaction processing system.

Choice "3" is incorrect. Executive information systems generally represent dashboard systems that provide macro-level information to executive leadership. Detailed decision support data to be generated by the system described for evaluating drilling sites does not meet the definition of an executive information system.

Choice "4" is incorrect. Management information systems are a type of business information system that provided managerial and other end-users with reports. Often reports are predetermined. Detailed decision support data to be generated by the system described for evaluating drilling sites does not meet the definition of a management information system.

QUESTION 3-1   FR-00755

Choice "3" is correct.

The assertions in statements I, III, and IV regarding ASP (Application Service Providers) are correct. Outsourcing application services do lower costs and provide greater flexibility. An ASP also runs security risks (lost control) but carries an advantage for smaller companies to avoid the high costs of maintaining a heavy IT infrastructure.

Statement II is incorrect. ASP costs are lower and not higher.

Choices "1", "2", and "4" are incorrect since they either inappropriately exclude one of the true statements or inappropriately include the incorrect statement.

Business IV

Topic C

QUESTION 1-1   FR-00763

Choice "2" is correct.

Security polices should seek to secure information as it is stored, processed or transmitted. Formatting is not a state or point at which information is safeguarded.

Choices "1", "3" and "4" are incorrect. Security policies should seek to secure information as it is stored, processed or transmitted.

QUESTION 4-1   FR-00761

Choice "4" is correct.

Encryption can be effective but, like most security measures, is not infallible.

Choice "1" is incorrect. The longer the length of the key and the more sophisticated the algorithm, the less likely that the message or transaction will be decrypted by the wrong party.

Choice "2" is incorrect. One of the most popular encryption methods uses a key length of 128 bits.

Choice "3" is incorrect. In a brute-force attack, the attacker simply tries every possible key until the right one is found.

QUESTION 4-2   FR-00196

Choice "1" is correct.

In this question, the examiners want to know which course of action is/are correct.

Statement I says that Landry should consider securing access to its mainframe computer room and moving its computer room to a convenient area right under its chemical mixing department. Landry should certainly consider securing access to its mainframe computer room, but it obviously should find another location for it. Statement I is incorrect.

Statement II says that Landry should consider implementing a new password protection scheme. Its current scheme provides no real protection at all. Statement II is correct.

Statement III says that Landry should consider implementing a file backup process to utilize the empty space right next to where the mainframe computer room might be moved. A permanent file backup process may be needed, but its location should not be right under the chemical mixing department. An offsite location should be considered. Statement III is incorrect.

Business IV

QUESTION 6-1 FR-00176

Choice "4" is correct.

In this question, the examiners want to know which, if any, of a series of statements is correct.

Statement I says that Conroe must have its disaster recovery plan certified by its external auditors. There is no such requirement. Statement I is incorrect.

Statement II says that Conroe's disaster recovery plan is more than sufficient given the nature of its business. Conroe's business is commodities trading and brokerage, and its disaster recovery plan is to reestablish processing at a cold site (where equipment has to be acquired) across the street. Conroe will be out of business by the time all that happens, even assuming that the "disaster" affected only its building and not the building across the street. Conroe needs a new Board of Directors. Statement II is incorrect.

Statement III says that Conroe's disaster recovery plan does not need to be tested because it will be relatively simple to transfer its data and programs to the cold site because it is so close. It will not be simple to transfer data that has been destroyed in the disaster or if the building across the street has been affected by the disaster. Testing will not improve this particular plan but, in general, all disaster recovery plans need to be tested. Statement III is incorrect.

QUESTION 6-2 FR-00758

Choice "3" is correct.

A cold site is an off-site location that has all the electrical connections and other physical requirements for data processing, but it does not have the actual equipment. Cold sites usually require one to three days to be made operational because equipment has to be acquired.

Choice "1" is incorrect. A warm backup site is a facility that is already stocked with all the hardware that it takes to create a reasonable facsimile of what you have in your primary data center.

Choice "2" is incorrect. A hot site is an off-site location that is equipped to take over the company's data processing.

Choice "4" is incorrect. This is not a type of offsite location.

Topic D

QUESTION 1-1   FR-00166

Choice "3" is correct.

In this question, the examiners want to know which of a series of controls might be reasonably required by the internal auditors of Macedonia Corporation.

Statement I is input controls that require that certain key data be validated. This type of control is certainly reasonable. It would be difficult to believe that some such controls are not already in place. Statement I is correct.

Statement II is input controls that require that all input data be processed in batches and that batch totals be maintained and verified for all batches. Input data is processed in batches in batch processing, (and batch totals are reasonable) but not necessarily in online processing. It would not be reasonable to apply batch processing concepts and procedures to an online environment if one existed. Statement II is incorrect.

Statement III is output controls that require that all reports be printed and manually distributed to end users through inter-office mail. Such a requirement might have been reasonable years ago, but not today. Today, many or most reports are distributed electronically and are never printed. Statement III is incorrect.

QUESTION 3-1   FR-00156

Choice "4" is correct.

In this question, the examiners want to know which, if any, of a series of statements is/are correct.

Statement I says that Lisa will not need a database administrator because the database management system will need no maintenance or support. All systems, including database management systems, need some kind of maintenance or support. Statement I is incorrect.

Statement II says that Lisa will need a data administrator to apply system upgrades to the database management system. Lisa will need someone to perform this function, but the person will be referred to as a database administrator, not a data administrator. Statement II is incorrect.

Statement III says that Lisa will not need any additional special expertise at all and that its existing programmers will be able to handle maintenance and support of the database management system. Lisa's existing programmers might be able to perform the maintenance and support function but more than likely would require special training to do so. Database management systems are very specialized and require special expertise. Statement III is incorrect.

Business IV

Topic E

Choice "4" is correct.

The faulty application of encryption could abort a transaction, but likely would not result in a faulty order.

Choice "1" is incorrect. The difficulty of authenticating the identity and, hence, the legitimacy of buyers and sellers is a major risk of e-commerce.

Choice "2" is incorrect. Maintaining privacy and confidentiality of information transmitted across public lines that might be compromised is a major risk of e-commerce.

Choice "3" is incorrect. Handling payment information from credit or banking sources is a major challenge in e-commerce.

Choice "1" is correct.

Older products possess less sophisticated security mechanisms. Legacy software was developed at a time when the understanding of the security "threatscape" was less advanced than the present. Many of the techniques developed by hackers to compromise systems, as well as strategies created by security professionals to protect them, were less mature in the past. Thus, this is a risk of a legacy system and is a reason to upgrade or implement a new system.

Choice "2" is incorrect. Vendors agreeing to continue ongoing support for a legacy system would be a reason in support for staying with the current system and would not be a reason in support of the change.

Choice "3" is incorrect. If special product customizations for every product are designed into a legacy system, this would be a reason in support for staying with the current system and would not be a reason in support of the change.

Choice "4" is incorrect. If the legacy system can run in any environment, this would be a reason in support for staying with the current system and would not be a reason in support of the change.

Business Final Review

Topic A

QUESTION 1-1

Choice "3" is correct.

Drivers would most likely comprehend nonfinancial measures that represent controllable features of their job. In this case, the achievement of a delivery within the time allowed (assuming standards properly consider miles and hours of service) would likely be the most effective metric.

Choice "1" is incorrect. Contribution per mile driven is a financial measure that would be useful for financial managers and even operational managers responsible for financial performance. This metric would not be as effective for drivers, as it does not relate to their job duties in a meaningful way.

Choice "2" is incorrect. Gross margin per mile driven is a financial measure that would be marginally useful since it comingles fixed and variable costs and uses a variable cost driver. However, the significance of the gross margin measure would most likely be lost on drivers.

Choice "4" is incorrect. Although beating standards is generally beneficial, using the wrong standards is potentially dangerous. If standards were computed properly in this instance, a driver could only beat them if he or she speeds or works longer than allowed by Department of Transportation regulations.

QUESTION 2-1

Choice "3" is correct.

ROI equals net income divided by average invested capital. Consequently, ROI equals 27.5% [($311,000 sales − $250,000 VC − $50,000 FC) / $40,000 average invested capital].

QUESTION 4-1

Choice "1" is correct.

Residual income is income of an investment center minus an imputed interest charge for invested capital. Accordingly, Vale's residual income is $144,000 [($500,000 sales − $300,000 VC − $50,000 traceable FC) net income − (6% × $100,000 average invested capital) imputed interest].

Business V

Topic B

FR-00193

Choice "2" is correct.

In this question, they want to know which of a series of statements about costs is/are correct. "All of the above" is an available option.

Statement I says that the cost of the raw materials in Applewhite's products is considered a variable cost. The more Applewhite manufactures, the more the total cost of the raw materials will be. Statement I is correct.

Statement II says that the cost of the depreciation of Applewhite's factory machinery is considered a variable cost because Applewhite uses an accelerated depreciation method for both book and income tax purposes. Just because a cost changes over time (which is what using an accelerated depreciation method will cause) does not mean that the cost is variable. The fact that Applewhite may use the same method for book and tax purposes is irrelevant. Statement II is wrong.

Statement III says that the cost of electricity for Applewhite's manufacturing facility is considered a fixed cost, even if the cost of the electricity has both variable and fixed components. The cost of the electricity would be considered a "mixed" cost, not a fixed cost. Statement III is wrong.

QUESTION 5-1

FR-00203

Choice "2" is correct.

In this question, they want to know the amount of overapplied or underapplied overhead at the end of a month.

For Culpepper, factory overhead is applied based on 40 percent of direct labor cost. Direct labor cost is $400,000, and factory overhead applied would be $160,000. Actual overhead is $175,000. Factory overhead would be underapplied by $15,000.

QUESTION 7-1   FR-00292

Choice "2" is correct.

The equivalent units of production for weighted average and FIFO are computed as follows:

FIFO

Beg. WIP [Percent **to be** completed; 100 × (1 − 60%)]		40
Units completed	500	
Beginning WIP	(100)	
		400
Ending WIP (Percent completed; 200 × 40%)		80
Equivalent Units		**520**

Weighted Average

Units completed	500
Ending WIP (Percent completed; 200 × 40%)	80
Equivalent Units	**580**

Choice "1" is incorrect. This selection identifies the computation of equivalent units with the wrong method.

Choice "3" is incorrect. This selection computes weighted average and FIFO equivalent units assuming that the percentage of ending inventory completion is consistent with the beginning of the month and, furthermore, reversed the presentation by placing FIFO under weighted average and vice versa.

Choice "4" is incorrect. This selection computes weighted average and FIFO equivalent units assuming that the percentage of ending inventory completion is consistent with the beginning of the month.

QUESTION 7-2   FR-00223

Choice "3" is correct.

In this question, they want a calculation of ending inventory cost using the weighted average method of process costing. The general approach to this problem is to (1) compute the equivalent units; (2) compute the unit cost of the production; and (3) apply the unit cost to the equivalent units in the ending inventory.

Before computing the equivalent units, it is helpful to reconcile the actual units. 100 units were in beginning inventory and 500 units were started, for a total of 600 units. 400 units were completed and 200 units remained in ending inventory, again for a total of 600 units.

Converting to equivalent units using the weighted-average method, the units completed at 100 percent complete and the units in ending inventory at their percentage of completion are considered. Equivalent units were thus 550 [400 + (200 × 0.75)]. Using the weighted average method, the percentage of completion of the beginning inventory is not considered.

To compute the unit cost of production, the cost of the beginning inventory plus the cost added during the month are considered. The cost of the beginning inventory was $50,000. $775,000 of cost was added during the month, for a total of $825,000 ($50,000 + $775,000). The per equivalent unit cost is $1,500 ($825,000 / 550).

There were 150 equivalent units in ending inventory (200 × 0.75). The cost of this inventory was thus $225,000 ($1,500 × 150).

Business Final Review

Business V

QUESTION 8-1

Choice "3" is correct.

In this question, they want to know which of a series of statements is/are correct with respect to ABC.

Statement I says that departmental costing systems are a refinement of ABC systems. Actually, ABC systems are a refinement of departmental costing systems. Statement I is incorrect.

Statement II says that ABC systems are useful in manufacturing, but not in merchandising or service industries. ABC systems are useful in all three of these businesses. Statement II is incorrect.

Statement III says that ABC systems can eliminate cost distortions because ABC develops cost drivers that have a cause-and-effect relationship with the activities performed. Statement III is correct.

QUESTION 9-1

Choice "2" is correct.

In this question, they want to know how much joint cost is allocated to each of two products. Joint cost allocation in this question is based on relative net realizable value (relative net sales value at split-off point), and sales values and separable costs after the split-off point are provided.

Using the relative net realizable value method of allocating joint costs, the net realizable value of both products can be calculated as follows:

	TomL	JimmyJ
Sales	$ 80,000	$ 50,000
Separable costs	(10,000)	(20,000)
Net realizable value	$ 70,000	$ 30,000

The joint cost is allocated based on the percentage of the product's net realizable value to the total. For TomL, that is 70% ($70,000 ÷ $100,000). 70% of the joint cost, or $140,000 ($200,000 × 0.70), is thus allocated to TomL.

30% of the joint cost, or $60,000 ($200,000 × 0.30), is allocated to JimmyJ, but they did not ask that.

QUESTION 9-2

Choice "2" is correct.

In this question, they want to know how much joint cost is allocated to each of two products. Joint cost allocation in this question is based on volume, and volumes are provided.

The total volume is 30,000 gallons. Product Astros has 20,000 gallons (2/3) of the total. Thus Product Astros is allocated $80,000 ($120,000 × 2/3) of the total, and Product Texans is allocated the remaining $40,000 ($120,000 × 1/3).

Topic C

QUESTION 3-1   FR-00818

Choice "3" is correct.

Failure demand is the demand for additional services due to the failure of the shared service operation to provide the proper level of service to the customer the first time. It can be viewed as "do over" work, because the inferior service (or product) must be provided again in order to satisfy the appropriate quality standards.

Choice "1" is incorrect. This concept applies to quality programs. Although there are proponents of zero-defect, even Six Sigma allows for some minor number of defects because a zero-defect standard is extremely difficult and costly to attain.

Choice "2" is incorrect. Although this situation might definitely occur, there is no name for it in process or product management.

Choice "4" is incorrect. Failure demand is not related to warranty programs.

QUESTION 5-1   FR-00817

Choice "3" is correct.

The concept of just-in-time (JIT) inventory systems is that resources will be introduced to the manufacturing process only as they are needed. An item is produced only when it is requested further downstream in the production cycle. JIT systems serve to make organizations more efficient and better managed.

Choice "1" is incorrect. Business process outsourcing involves contracting with a third party to provide a service, such as accounts payable or payroll operations. Risks pertaining to outsourcing services include inferior quality of service and the security of information, which may be compromised.

Choice "2" is incorrect. Shared services is a consolidation of redundant services within an organization or group of affiliates. While consolidation of redundant services leads to efficiency, it may result in service flow disruption.

Choice "4" is incorrect. DMAIC is a methodology of Six Sigma that is applied to existing product and business process improvements. It stands for **D**efine the problem, **M**easure key aspects of the current process, **A**nalyze data, **I**mprove or optimize current processes, and **C**ontrol.

Topic D

QUESTION 1-1   FR-00265

Choice "1" is correct.

In this question, they want to know the operating income using a flexible budget. Certain actual and static budget data for the company is provided. The flexible budget will be for the actual 24,000 units.

The fixed costs for the flexible budget for the 24,000 units actually produced were the same as the static (master) budget for the 20,000 units, or $60,000. The variable costs will have to be converted to a per unit basis. Variable costs were 60% of sales ($120,000 / $200,000), or $6 per unit (the unit sales price of $10 × 0.60), with a contribution margin of 40% of sales or $4 per unit. At sales of 24,000 units, the contribution margin was $96,000 ($4 × 24,000). Subtracting the fixed costs produces a net income of $36,000 ($96,000 − $60,000).

Business V

Choice "4" is correct.

Sales forecasts are used as a basis for developing sales budgets. The sales budget drives the anticipated volume of production and needed capacity that is used for anticipating expenses.

Choice "1" is incorrect. Variance analysis is possible using a master budget. Although the results of variance analysis using a master budget may be distorted and therefore less useful as a result of differences in volume, variance analysis is not impossible using a master budget.

Choice "2" is incorrect. Master budgets are, indeed, generally and almost always developed on an annual basis, but the may be developed for different periods. The predominant characteristic of master budgets and other techniques is that it assumes one level of activity.

Choice "3" is incorrect. A flexible budget is not based on standards so much as it is based on different levels of activity. The flexible budget may act as a basis for developing standards, however, the flexible budget, in and of itself, does not create standards associated with required output for allowed output.

Choice "2" is correct.

In this question, they want to know which, if any, of a series of statements is/are correct. "All of the above" is an available option.

Statement I says that master budgets are normally confined to a single year for a single level of activity. Statement I is correct.

Statement II says that flexible budgets are financial plans prepared in a manner that allows for adjustments for changes in production or sales and accurately reflects expected costs for the adjusted output. Statement II is the definition of flexible budgets. Statement II is correct.

Statement III says that, normally, the first step in the preparation of Bronx's master budget for a year would be the preparation of its production budget. However, before the production budget can be prepared, a sales budget is needed. Statement III is incorrect.

Statement IV says that the success of Bronx's budgeting program will depend on the degree to which its top management accepts the program and how its management uses the budgeted data. Statement IV is correct.

Choice "3" is correct.

The problem requires the candidate to derive budgeted cash payments for the month of May from a series of assumptions provided by the budget. The components included in May's sales were assembled in April and purchased in March. Purchases were paid 75% in the month of purchase and 25% following the month of purchase. The cash budget for May would represent the 75% of the purchases in May and 25% of the purchases in April. May purchases relate to June assembly of July sales. April purchases relate to May assembly of June sales. ($8,000 × 75% + $7,000 × 25% = $7,750)

Business V

QUESTION 4-1

Choice "1" is correct.

In this question, they want to know the materials usage variance for a particular product. Certain data for the product is provided.

In this particular question, 8,400 pounds of material were used. 2,000 units of Brook were produced. The standard usage for 2,000 units was 8,000 pounds (2,000 × 4). The standard price was $2.50 per pound. Because the actual usage was greater than the standard usage, the materials usage variance must be unfavorable.

The variance formula for the materials usage variance can be stated as the standard price of $2.50 times the difference between the actual and standard usage of 400 pounds (8,400 − 8,000), or $1,000 (*unfavorable*).

QUESTION 4-2

Choice "4" is correct.

In this question, they want to know the labor rate variance for a particular product. Certain data for the product is provided.

In this question, 9,500 hours of labor were worked to produce the 2,500 units of the broadband router. The actual rate of the labor was thus $11 per hour ($104,500 / 9,500), slightly above the standard rate. Thus, any labor rate variance is going to have to be unfavorable.

The standard for the 9,500 hours worked to produce the 2,500 units was $95,000 (9,500 ×$10). The difference between the actual of $104,500 and the standard of $95,000 was $9,500.

Another way to work the same question is to use the formula. The variance formula for the labor rate variance can be stated as the actual hours worked times the difference between the actual and standard rates [9,500 × ($11 − $10)], or $9,500 (*unfavorable*).

QUESTION 4-3

Choice "2" is correct.

In this question, they want to know the variable overhead spending variance for a product. Certain data for the product are provided.

The actual hours used to produce the 4,000 units of Bedford were 8,200 hours, and the standard hours to produce 4,000 units were 8,000 hours. Variable overhead is based on labor hours. The actual variable overhead rate is $5.10 ($41,820 / 8,200).

The variance formula for the variable overhead spending variance can be stated as the actual hours of 8,200 hours times the difference between the actual and standard rates of $.10 ($5.10 − $5.00), or $820 (*unfavorable*).

Business V

Choice "3" is correct.

In this question, they want to know which of a series of statements is/are correct for a responsibility accounting system. "None of the above" is not an available option, and neither is "All of the above."

Statement I says that, in a cost SBU, managers are responsible for controlling costs but not revenue. Statement I is correct.

Statement II says that the idea behind responsibility accounting is that a manager should be held responsible for those items, and only those items, that the manager can actually control to a significant extent. Statement II is correct.

Statement III says that, to be effective, a good responsibility accounting system must provide for both planning and control. Planning without control and control without planning is not effective. Statement III is correct.

Statement IV says that common costs that are allocated to a SBU are normally controllable by the SBU's management. Common costs that are allocated are normally not controllable by an SBU's management. Statement IV is incorrect.

QUESTION 6-1 FR-00184

Choice "4" is correct.

In this question, they want to know which of a series of statements is/are correct.

Statement I says that a balanced scorecard reports management information regarding organizational performance in achieving goals classified by critical success factors to demonstrate that no single dimension of organizational performance can be relied upon to evaluate success. This statement is the definition of a balanced scorecard. Statement I is correct.

Statement II says that performance measures used in a balanced scorecard tend to be divided into financial, customer, internal business process, and learning and growth. Statement II is correct.

Statement III says that, in a balanced scorecard, internal business processes are what the company does in its attempts to satisfy customers. Statement III is correct.

Topic E

QUESTION 1-1 FR-00261

Choice "1" is correct.

The contribution margin from manufacturing (sales − variable costs) is $10 ($40 − $30) per unit sold, or $1,200,000 (120,000 units × $10). The fixed costs of manufacturing ($600,000) and selling and administrative costs ($400,000) are deducted from the contribution margin to arrive at an operating income of $200,000. The difference between the absorption income and the variable costing income is attributable to capitalization of the fixed manufacturing costs under the absorption method. Since 40% of the goods produced are still in inventory (80,000 / 200,000), 40% of the $600,000 in fixed costs, or $240,000, was capitalized under the absorption method. That amount was expensed under the variable costing method.

Business V

QUESTION 2-1   FR-00163

Choice "2" is correct.

The question requires computation of the breakeven point in dollars for a product. Certain cost and other data are provided.

Annual sales are $900,000, and the sales price is $20 per unit. That means 45,000 units were sold. $900,000 is one of the answers, but it cannot be the correct answer because there was a profit of $2 per unit and the question is asking for breakeven.

On a unit basis, total fixed overhead was $10 ($7 + $3). At 45,000 units, total fixed costs were $450,000.

To determine the breakeven point, it is necessary to determine the variable cost per unit. Prime cost (direct materials and direct labor) is given, and so are variable overhead and variable selling and administrative costs. Total variable costs are thus $8 ($6 + $1 + $1).

The breakeven equation for this question can be written as $20X = 8X + 450,000$, where X is the units sold at the breakeven point. Solving for X produces 37,500 units at $20 per unit, or $750,000 ($20 × 37,500).

Note: An alternative approach is to divide the total fixed costs by the contribution margin percentage. Fixed costs are $450,000. The contribution margin (sales minus variable costs) is $20 − $8 = $12. The contribution margin percentage is $12 / $20 = 60%. Fixed costs of $450,000 / 60% = $750,000.

QUESTION 5-1   FR-00291

Choice "3" is correct.

Harbor would compare its variable costs of production and relevant (avoidable) fixed costs ($4.50). Costs are comprised of direct labor and direct material of $2.00 and the variable factory overhead of $1.00 along with avoidable fixed costs of $1.50 ($15,000/10,000) to arrive at total relevant costs of $4.50. Harbor would buy the bolts since its relevant production costs are greater than the proposed purchase price.

Choice "1" is incorrect. Harbor would need to consider more than its prime costs as part of the analysis.

Choice "2" is incorrect. Harbor would need to consider more than its variable costs as part of the analysis.

Choice "4" is incorrect. Harbor would not consider irrelevant fixed costs as part of the analysis.

QUESTION 8-1   FR-00277

Choice "1" is correct.

Simple linear regression involves only one independent variable. Multiple linear regression analysis involve more than one independent variable.

Choice "2" is incorrect. Multiple linear regression analysis analyzes the impact of multiple independent variables (income, competitors, etc.) on a single dependent variable (revenue) not vice versa.

Choice "3" is incorrect. While non-linear multiple regression analysis may consider the dynamic relationships associated with multiple independent and dependent variables, multiple linear regression only considers the impact of multiple independent variables on a single dependent variable.

Choice "4" is incorrect. This is a distracter. Codependence has more to do with psychoanalysis than regression analysis.

Business Final Review   **CQ-33**

Business V

QUESTION 9-1   FR-00214

Choice "4" is correct.

In this question, they want to know which statement is correct with respect to regression analysis. The only given fact is that there is a 0.90 correlation coefficient between the variables X and Y.

Statement I says that there is little relationship between X and Y. The correlation coefficient is the strength of the relationship between the independent and dependent variables X and Y. Because correlation coefficients range between –1.00 and 1.00, a correlation coefficient of 0.90 would indicate a strong relationship. Statement I is incorrect.

Statement II says that variation in X explains 90% of the variation in Y. This statement is discussing the coefficient of determination, not the correlation coefficient. Statement II is incorrect.

Statement III says that, if X increases, Y will never decrease. If the correlation were perfect with a correlation coefficient of 1.00, "never" would be correct. Statement III is incorrect.

Statement IV says that, if X increases, Y will generally increase. Statement IV is correct.

QUESTION 11-1   FR-00143

Choice "2" is correct.

In this question, they want to know the cost function from a set of data for units and costs using the high-low method.

The high level is the 1,900 units in February, and the low level is the 1,100 units in July. The costs for those months are $15,200 and $12,800. None of the other months are relevant because the high-low method uses only the high and low months.

The slope of the line is the change in cost of $2,400 ($15,200 − $12,800) divided by the change in activity of 800 (1,900 − 1,100), or $3 per unit.

The total cost of $15,200 less the variable cost of $5,700 for those units ($3 × 1,900), yields fixed cost of $9,500.